Stock Market Mistakes

by

Matthew Giannino

ISBN 978-1-7345540-6-9 (paperback)
ISBN 978-1-7345540-7-6 (e-book)
ISBN 978-1-7345540-8-3 (audiobook)

MARKET MOVES LLC
8781 Sheridan Blvd #6046
Westminster, CO 80003

www.marketmovesmatt.com

FINANCIAL DISCLAIMER

Market Moves LLC and Matt Giannino is a company that provides education in financial and stock market literacy. WE ARE NOT FINANCIAL ADVISORS. In fact, it is illegal for us to provide any financial advice to you. Under U.S. law, the only persons who can give you financial advice are those who are licensed financial advisors through the SEC. We hold no such licenses, and therefore, if you ask for financial advice, we will simply direct you to speak with your professional financial advisor. Our mission is simply to provide you with some of the educational tools to help you navigate the stock market, thereby enabling you (with the help of your financial advisor) to make better decisions with your money. Results shown from Market Moves LLC, Matt Giannino, or customers who use our product and/or service are individual experiences, reflecting real life experiences. These are individual results and results do vary. Market Moves LLC and Matt Giannino does not claim that they are typical results that consumers will generally achieve. The testimonials are not necessarily representative of all of those who will use our products and/or services. Past performance does not guarantee future results. You should not rely on any past performance as a guarantee of future investment performance

CONTENTS

ABOUT MARKET MOVES
- MATT GIANNINO

F eel free to skip this part - if you don't want to hear how I started trading, lost it all, quit my job for it, turned accounts from $3,000 to $25,000 multiple times in just a couple of months, $40k to $200k (pictured below), teach hundreds how to trade daily, and most importantly found my passion in life.

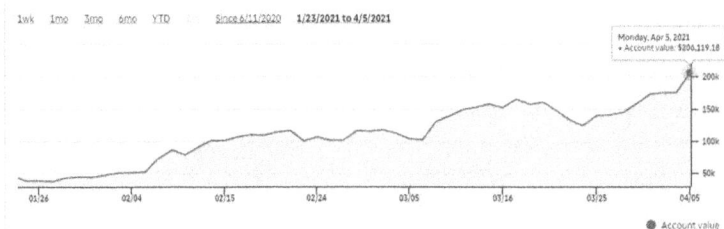

As you may know, I am or was a professional runner, depending on when you are reading this book. But back in 2016 after my first stress fracture, I used that time to become obsessed with another hobby called Day Trading the Stock Market. For someone working a part-time job that paid very little, this seemed like a very dangerous and risky way to spend my free time. I mean, I knew very little to nothing about trading stocks. One of the main reasons I was attracted to it was a conversation I heard between my Dad and Nick (Topanga - Don't Ask...). Back in Boston after skipping my race because I was obviously too injured to run, they were rambling about the stock market and how everything was beaten up and had plenty of room to run. This amazed me, seeing my Dad and my best friend Nick so excited and passionate about a subject I knew very little about.

Nick obviously was very interested in trading the stock market day-to-day while my Dad was giving us advice about investing long term. Everything I heard perked my ears up and moved some rusty gears in my brain. The rest is really history; from that day I dove into stocks and started trading with everything I had (literally). This is very common for me, I have an all-or-nothing mentality. With all this new free time, I was especially all-in now that I could not run and had to find other ways to make my time productive. Running has really let me down lately and now is the time to increase my knowledge or skills somewhere else. Always keep growing is my mantra and if you stop growing you are dying. It is basically science; I mean what else is the point of this life other than to make the most of it? Become a better person every day and constantly throw yourself into the depths of change. That's what I did.

That cold winter in 2016 I spent almost all my time watching CNBC, going to Barnes and Noble's reading books, and waiting for myself to heal. It was a dark and wonderful time. I started trading with $3,000. For the first 90 days, I would not have to pay trading fees so luckily I was really experimenting in the market. During that time, the market was going up every day and I could only buy stocks, so I felt like a genius. My portfolio was up 50% easily in the first couple of weeks. How would I not be good at trading when stocks rocketed higher every day? I mean they were coming off very low levels and finally popping! The fact that I could only go long made it easier for me to make money. Obviously, this was not enough, having this early success, I wanted to learn more. I stumbled upon options trading not long after being in the market. This is possibly one of the riskiest ways to trade the stock market, most options expire (or become) worthless, which means there are unlimited ways to lose money. But I loved the fact that I could gain leverage from them. If I picked a trade properly instead of making 3%, I could make 80-100%. Why would I not take the options trading? If you guess it, it did not take long before my impressive gains withered away to nothing. Literally nothing, I ended up losing everything in my portfolio trading those options. Of course, I did, I had no rules, no structure. The market has no structure. If you mix those things with no structure, it is bound to end in a total financial loss.

So I took some time and rethought my strategy to try and understand how much more money I could risk in the market, and then I dove back in. I just got a couple of paychecks and took a week's breather from trading. I realized my mistakes with these foreign derivatives called options trading and moved on. I think now is the time to restart and try again. Not long after that, the same thing happened; I stumbled hard and sent another account to zero. Amazing! During this time of healing my injured body, I am also subjecting myself to financial losses. It was miserable but I went back to the library and the internet to learn more and more and more. I knew the long-term benefit of understanding the stock market and I didn't want to give up on it. I mean tons of people owe $80,000 in student loans. I just paid $4,000 to the trading university. Seemed like a cheaper education in my opinion. One day I may have $50,000 or even $1,000,000 and at that point, I may see my portfolio swinging $4,000 a day. Long term I saw the light, I saw the possibility. I knew that this was a chump change compared to what I was going to be doing in the future. So that justified using this money as learning money. At the end of the day money really doesn't mean anything, life is short. I don't want to put much emphasis on being rich. I really just want to develop skills, especially skills that can make me financially free.

This has already been a long ramble on my back story to trading. Fast forward to 2019, and everything had changed. Everything! Good and bad. I spent the next three years trading the markets on and off. On and off meaning I would lose everything, wait a couple of weeks or months, deposit some more, and try again. I attempted trading the markets many times. Options were really hard. If you had poor risk management which I had, it was almost impossible to keep any streak going. 2017 ended with huge losses on my tax return. 2018 started off on a bad note but ended much differently. Obviously, my negative momentum from 2017 to 2018 led me to lose some money early in 2018. But once I started investing in the summer in stocks and crypto, everything changed. I started my portfolio out with $12,000 and months later I found it at $25,000. This return was unreal to me and my options strategy and crypto strategy were finally working. It felt amazing and I was really killing it. I was so confident that I found the strategy and my purpose/passion in life, and I finally quit my part-time job. This was where I taught after-school engineering classes and got paid 40 bucks a day. It took about 3 hours and I had to manage 10-20 kids playing. This was also my third year with the company and it was time for a change. I just want to say I had an amazing time meeting all these co-workers, the job gave me the ultimate freedom (I rarely saw my boss, I basically was my own boss), and I really did it as a means to give back my knowledge of engineering to kids. 90% of the time I tried to pour my soul into those classes, helping those kids learn, have more confidence in themselves and have fun most importantly. It taught me a lot, teaching people, interacting with kids, and being comfortable managing people. These skills will help me out in 2018-2019 just wait (full circle).

So my confidence in trading and investing led me to quit, buy a huge TV as a monitor and try full-time trading from home. Yeah, I bet you are cringing right now. It seemed like the universe was leading me, so I listened and followed.

The signs were there honestly. Not to mention that right before I quit, I shorted the overall market for the first time ever right before the biggest pullback in 10 years. Yeah, again, confidence was high....too high. So I ended up day trading from home for the first month. At the back of my mind, I knew that this freedom was a little too dangerous and if not managed properly would be bad for me. The big reason I could trade and have more freedom was that if my account is above $25k I am allowed to trade AS MUCH AS I WANT. Sorry to not mention that part, so that extra freedom was what I was talking about when I said I needed to balance it properly. But as I said before, I had no risk management and no rules. I was still bound to fail in the long run according to most trading books I read, so all these changes and being able to make unlimited trades were coupled with trying to trade futures. This basically was like starting a fire at the gas stations. I was bound to blow up in the worst way.

So futures are basically a derivative different from options in the sense that your losses are not limited. Meaning you could lose way more than you put in.....ouch. If you think this sounds awful you are right. Oh yeah, I also didn't mention that because the market dropped the largest amount in the last ten years this jacked up the volatility to insane levels. This means that you make a lot of money quickly and lose a lot of money quickly. These levels were 1 to 3% moves a day in the index when the average was only under 0.3%. It was the most dangerous time to be investing in futures. But I went right in as I do and tried to learn the good and bad lessons first hand. In the first couple of days, good momentum carried my account to 28k. And shortly after that, my account dropped below 25k which is the threshold you need to have to trade as much as you can. So that was tough and added some pressure to trade my way back above 25k. The market was climbing day by day and I was holding onto my 2 futures positions losing thousands of dollars. Every day I would wake up and it kept rising. My account was slowly shrinking and was under 15k at this point. I was fully expecting the market to drop hard and enter a bear market, the super bear market everyone has been waiting for but it didn't. Just when I sold all my positions to cut my losses and ended the bleeding my account was at 13k, which was almost half of what it was when I started. This was too devastating so I vowed to stay away from futures and decided to take a break.

Shortly after I sold, the market did sell off a large amount, the move I was waiting for. If I held everything my account would have jumped to 50k. Letting me learn the most obvious lesson, right after you sell is when your move happens. This happens all the time. During this time of trading, I became a little too obsessed and it definitely took away from my running. If I held any positions overnight I would not be able to sleep which cuts down on recovery from training obviously. During this time I still managed to run a 3:43 1500m and a 1:52 800m personal record in track. Oh yeah, you probably forgot I was still professionally running, and actually healthy now. So I still could balance both but I would be lying if I said trading didn't take a toll on running in some way or another.

Fast forward one more time to the latter half of 2018 after getting married. During this time I started a YouTube channel which grew to more than 1,000 subscribers enough to get paid by YouTube daily. I can attribute this idea and success to Gary Vee. He is an online influencer who preaches putting content on the internet (DOCUMENTING), which is what I am doing. So I listened to him and now I have one form of passive income and slowly adding more social channels. My goal is to eventually be a trading online influencer sharing my skills and trades daily. I started trading on Robinhood because it was a free platform where plenty of millennials went to invest. The YouTube search was through the roof for Robinhood videos. It was crazy. So I went to this platform just to dabble in investing and show others how to trade, etc.

Only a month later did I buy put options on TLRY while it is climbing to 300 and then in the flash of an eye drops to 150$. It was crazy, I was involved in the most profitable day trade in history I would say and I was buying this at the exact top. This quadrupled my $3,000 account all the way up to $12,000. It was mind-blowing. The momentum from that led me to get my account to $25,000. Once again over the day trading limit. Now I was back in business I could trade full time again. No more restrictions. The freedom was back...but could I handle it? This in the meantime was all live on YouTube, the trades, the progress. I was displaying it to the world. I would wake up and show my users how to make $1,000 in 15 minutes. I made a $3k to $50 challenge on YouTube and slowly brought my account to $46k!! Every day I woke up, I kept making money and I was seeing my account grow in a way I didn't think was possible. I was in the zone. Sometimes I would stretch a little too far and lose a big portion, like 5-7k. And have to put myself back in check and be smarter. Then one day I hit 46k and I wanted nothing more than to hit 50k in front of all my viewers and complete the challenge.

Fast forward to 2021, I was able to grow my account from $40,000 to $200,000 in a matter of 2 months selling options and trading one stock. I decided it was time to pay myself and for the first time ever trading, I took out $100k profit, which really gives you a good idea of the journey. We tend to sweat the small stuff, in the beginning, losing $3,000, and we forget the possibilities. I knew from day one of trading the money I could make would greatly triumph the money I could lose my first couple of years. The only factor on when traders can make this transition is based on their ability to control themselves and avoid the mistakes we are going to mention in this book. It may take a lifetime if you cannot put a system in place to limit risk and control emotions. But if that system works, that is when this game gets exciting.

Nowadays, what I spend most of my time on is trading, a big surprise. I also post content on YouTube every week teaching traders everything they need to know, as well as offering free courses on my website. I also learned an important lesson after making $40,000 in 2 months, that money without people is loneliness. It sucks. That is why I share my options trades and setups with a premium trading group every week. This is the best of all worlds; I can trade, teach, and connect with some amazing people.   I would love to buy you 7 days into my group, no cost for you. Just click the link here: https://www.marketmovesmatt.com/trade-alert-special

HOW TO USE THIS BOOK

These mistakes are actual dollar mistakes that will be placed on your tuition bill. The goal of trading is to make that tuition bill as small as possible. Failing small and failing fast is the goal of learning anything in life. As a brand new trader that should be your mantra. Get that 1000% YOLO garbage out of your head, this book was strictly written for those who want to make this their full time job, those who want the ability to conquer their mind, emotions, and perfect a killer strategy. You have to honestly ask yourself right now, have you ever pushed through anything in life and been consistent until you reached success. If you are married, do you commit yourself to being the best spouse every single day? Have you ran a marathon, have you hiked to the top of a mountain, have you finished school, or have you finished anything meaningful that was a struggle? My point is, you are going to struggle to do this and if you haven't developed resilience or perseverance somewhere else in your life, you are most likely going to give up on this. This is hard and all these mistakes I am going to list are going to test your willpower daily in the stock market.

So if you don't have something in life you can say you gave 100% and pushed through the struggles, MAKE THIS THAT THING. This is your chance to reverse that pattern of giving up in life when things aren't as fun as you thought they were, when things weren't as easy as WallStreetBets perceived them. Promising yourself you will commit to this one thing will enhance everything else in your life. You will find yourself committing more as a parent, friend, spouse, and more. Rise to the occasion by accepting the challenge, looking at these mistakes we all will make, and know they are coming. Make yourself aware of all these mistakes so when they happen you can acknowledge them. Move forward and find ways to redefine your strategies, to stop the mistakes in the future. The goal of trading is not, to never lose, never fail, or never get emotional. The goal of trading is to limit the number of times we lose and limit the downside when we do. Understand our emotions and become more familiar with how to deal with them.

THIS APPLIES TO
EVERYTHING

T he lessons I'm going to talk about inside this book reference many trading mistakes. I am writing these from my first-hand experience. Like many people getting started in the stock market, they tend to make all the mistakes possible. They can only learn from first-hand experience. I believe I was prepared to succeed in the stock market because I spent most of my life running competitively. The lessons I learned in running are very similar to the lessons I learned in the stock market. The mindset, the mistakes, the path to success, is all very similar. As it is with anything where we are striving for greatness and putting ourselves out there. Accomplishing something big and scary requires a tremendous amount of hard work, dedication, perseverance, consistency, and more. I practice this every single day in trading and I learned this through my time running competitively. Throughout this book, I will reference specific mistakes I made running, and show

how those mistakes parallel in the stock market. This is meant to show you that these lessons are universal. You can apply them to many different places inside your life. They should not be limited or confined to just stock market mistakes. As you know from my story previously, I started out trading the stock market with no prior knowledge. I had zero clues what technical analysis meant. My parents didn't work at a hedge fund. I didn't know what a dividend was. Just a couple of years later, I was able to withdraw $100,000 (PROFIT) from my trading account. This was only possible through sheer perseverance and dedication. I would not have been able to do this if I hadn't learned the same qualities and lessons through my running career.

Just like trading, I started out running with no prior experience. My parents weren't Olympians and I had no idea who Prefontaine was. In my first year running, I decided to watch the Olympics and saw an American get a silver medal in the 1500 meters. This is my first time ever competing in the sport and ever watching the sport. This lit a flame inside me, as well as many other things in the next 10 years, to continue to strive and find out what my body was capable of. In the 10th year of running competitively, I ended up running the 1500 meters with that silver medalist. That same Olympian that lit the spark inside me to be great was standing right next to me on the starting line. I could never live up to his resume, but being at that race next to him we were almost equals. My hard work and everything I sacrificed (which was a lot) had finally felt validated. That silver medalist I looked up to, we ended up bumping shoulders in the final straightaway of our race. I realized that by committing myself to excellence and seeing one thing though, anything was possible. It is not a coincidence it took ten years to reach this moment in running. The idea is, 10,000 hours of dedicated practice which comes out to about 10 years. It takes ten years to master anything and there are no shortcuts. You're the only person standing in front of yourself. So throughout this book, I will reference the lessons I learned from running and trading because those are the two things I've committed myself to becoming great at. I'm telling you this now because I am not someone who talks the talk. I really value actually putting up results and talking less. I've made more money than I've lost in the stock market. I have raced Olympians who I used to look up to on TV. So I appreciate you letting me share my journey as an attempt to give you an idea of what you're in for. What you may need to overcome to achieve your goals in life.

CONTROLLING LETHAL EMOTIONS

You wake up in the morning, the stock you believe in so much just did a share offering, and it is now tanking pre-market. You believe in the company but you can't believe it just dropped. Even before the market opens your emotions are running high. You already see red in your portfolio just from the stock alone, and you have long-term options on it as well. You know when the market opens those are going to be deep red too. That opening bell hits, the loss you're seeing in the first three seconds is more disgusting than you ever expected waking up. The loss aversion mindset starts running like the energizer bunny. Trying to come up with a dozen ways for you to make up that money as quickly as possible. The little devil on your left shoulder gives you the idea of playing zero-day options with the SPY. That should be the easiest way to make back those losses. You're angry and emotional. You don't even wait for a good entry point, you know the markets are going to drop so you just fire away on some puts. That trade goes read instantly but you don't care. You know you can't be wrong twice so you add to the position a little bit more. Ten minutes later, you realize the setup you spotted earlier for the SPY was completely wrong. You messed up everything about this trade, coming in hot, entering without a plan, just based on the emotions driven from that morning loss. To make things even worse, the stock that had an offering actually goes back to yesterday's price, and all the money you saw that was red as an unrealized loss actually disappears. You think to yourself, "Dang if I just woke up five minutes past the market open I would have missed all of this and I wouldn't have entered this dumb trade for the SPY." So you let your emotions control you. You woke up in the morning and saw red, and panicked like chicken little, "The Sky Is Falling!" This panic drove you to make an unnecessary trade which resulted in a loss. Had you not panicked, your account would be flat, as the initial stock drop came back. This is teaching you one of the best lessons of all times, which is, sometimes, no trade is better than a forced trade.

Anything I'm writing in this book has definitely been a personal experience. I'm sure I've done all these 3 to 4 times this year alone. Controlling emotions, even if you are a seasoned trader, is something that is extremely tough to do. Controlling emotions as a new trader is next to impossible. You have to work every single day to understand these emotions, realize reactions to them, and come up with a plan to minimize those reactions. Note, how I didn't say eliminate. That is just not possible because we are irrational and imperfect humans. Every single loss traders make in the stock market is driven by their emotions. Controlling those emotions is how we avoid those massive mistakes. This takes so long to master. The whole book honestly should be about how to do this. I'm going to do my best to list some of the key lethal emotions you have to recognize because you won't be able to control them if you can't recognize them.

LETHAL EMOTION #1
FOMO/JEALOUSY

Lethal emotion number one, FOMO (the fear of missing out), is that feeling you get when you're sick to your stomach and you realize you missed the trade you planned out and spent so much time getting ready for. You see it working out instantly, 30% out of the gate. It's also caused by spending any amount of time on social media or in a chat group. Everyone is making money on RKT today. If everyone's making money why can't you? You missed out, you want to find something to give you that sweet satisfaction of making money. So you're no longer the one being left out. So you rush to find another quick setup that can make money. You rush the whole process because the stock market took your favorite setup from you, leaving you no time to get in. When you feel FOMO, it is so important to understand that you feel it. I understand this urge to be a part of the play or to be a part of a group of people making money. But it's super unhealthy for your account. You have to trust the long game. Giving up profits today is not a big deal, considering the fact that you can make money every single day in the stock market. You could possibly make money every single second in the crypto market as it trades 24/7. So why worry about one setup or one trade. Have some faith that if you found a great trade, you could find another one again. There's an opportunity every single day if you prepare yourself for it. It certainly sucks missing out. We're hardwired inside our bodies to want to be a part of something. The best way to avoid this feeling is to walk away. Tell yourself you're not gonna force a trade. Put in the work to find the next best thing. Be patient, don't rush it.

LETHAL EMOTION
#2 GREED

S o you finally started making money in the stock market and you are crushing your goal of 50 bucks a day. Instead of being bored and consistently profiting, you think there has to be more to this. You decide to shoot for 100 bucks a day. This means you're doubling your position size to get those higher profits on every single trade. Maybe you're jealous of seeing someone buy a Lamborghini. Maybe one of your friends from high school made $40,000 in bitcoin. You could be content with putting food on the table or the ability to pay your mortgage, which most people consider a successful life. You decide it's not enough and you need more. You need that extra $40K from bitcoin profits to purchase that Lamborghini and compete with those idiots on Instagram. You need to trade Gamestop because you don't want to feel left out from everyone making millions of dollars. You just need to make more money. This is extreme greed, needing to do something in the stock market. It also never ends well.

We all have this emotion. We are not superheroes. It's fueled by a number of other things inside this book. What I've learned from my years of trading the stock market is when you're reaching for more money or pushing for your account to hit a certain level; that is when you are opening yourself up to maximum risk. I remember thinking about this twice in my crazy trading career. I was making consistent money for a couple straight months. Everything was easy. I was on fire. I looked at my account, and I thought, "Wouldn't it be cool to see double this amount?" Grow a $25,000 account to $50,000, or a $50,000 account to $100,000. If I could just double right now I would be complete, dare I say, happy. I've also thought this way in trade; I would put $10,000 into a trade, and think about the outcome right away. If I'm able to double this, I can make $10,000 on my $10,000. Greed is the cartoon money signs in your eyes. It's when you stop being content and start driving for bigger and better.

From my experience in the past when you're striving for a certain number or a certain profit you're also reaching. The act of reaching is 100% fueled by greed, and any lethal emotion driving decisions will blur all those rules you learned over the last couple of years trading. The emotions we are talking about inside this book are going to be the emotions that blur everything you've learned inside this book. The emotions force you to forget your rules. This book will be totally worthless unless you realize these emotions need to be controlled as best as you can. If you can control yourself, trading becomes much easier. I can tell you from the past, trying to do big things with your account involves taking on big position size. This means if you're wrong, it's going to result in a big loss. Just like we said before, the stock market is a marathon, and it takes a while to get good at it. Like any marathon, it's about pacing yourself, being slow and steady. Just like trading, just like adding up your profits, slow and steady. Just execute and lock it in.

LETHAL EMOTION
#3 ANGER

I t seems silly that anger is a lethal emotion we have to battle within ourselves because of the stock market. Unfortunately, it is one of those unavoidable things that is extremely natural for humans to feel in certain situations. Like many of these lethal emotions, they are the root cause of any of the mistakes we will list throughout this book. Therefore, it is very important we point them out early and you identify them in your own trading as they appear. Anger is triggered by trading for a couple of reasons. As a trader, we tend to become attached to two things, our money and our ideas. Being attached to anything in life is dangerous. Since our trading group is Star Wars themed I will throw in some quotes from the movie. "Attachment leads to jealousy, the shadow of greed, that is." "Fear leads to anger, anger leads to hate, and hate leads to suffering." Let's discuss the first attachment of money. Money is something people are naturally attached to. Studies have shown that when a person loses money, it is one of the most painful feelings they can go through. When we lose money in the stock market, this naturally makes us very angry. This is one of the main igniters of this emotion. Another anger trigger is being wrong about their ideas. As traders, we put in an awful amount of hard work and research. Trading, in general, is hard and feels impossible in the beginning. We study and perfect trading indicators, stocks, concepts, and more. We finally feel like we made sense from something that makes no sense. We spend hours charting, planning, and then finally executing. As we get closer to finding great setups in the stock market, we become attached to them once we find them. It is hard work.

You know triangles are bullish. You studied this company for years. You have every right to be excited about this opportunity. If you weren't excited, you wouldn't be doing this. But when we are in the trade, we forget the fact that anything can happen, good and bad. All that hard work put in, leads to you being that much more attached to it. This also means you feel that much more terrible when the market does the opposite. Trust me; I have seen it all. You are scalping the market in the quickest time frame. You made 50% on trade and are about to take profit. Then the president talks about raising taxes and the market drops like a rock within seconds. 50% gains turn into 50% losses. That sucks! There is no better way to say that. We bust our butts to make a dollar; once we have it, the market takes it away instantly. You find a great company to buy long term that nobody realizes is a great opportunity. You study the company every night, getting excited about their future, growing more and more attached to it. This makes it that much more aggravated when the stock keeps dropping because the hedge funds don't see what you do. We have to do a better job of accepting the fact that anything can happen no matter how great our setup or research was. We need to shift from being attached towards knowing we can be wrong and we can lose money in the stock market. The stock market is a cruel beast that was created to take your money. It knows every trick in the book how to release these lethal emotions so you give up even more.

LETHAL EMOTION #4 FEAR

Y ou just started trading and find the thought of losing money overwhelming. You obviously came here to make money, but if your account turns red, you are not sure what will happen next. This money is meaningful to you. You would rather use it to buy a new car. Your friends convince you that the money you could buy a Lamborghini with is better invested in Mooncoin. You are hesitant, but people all around you are making money so you are less worried. As you put your whole bank account in Mooncoin, you constantly lose sleep every night. You get sick at the thought of losing that money. You are afraid and nervous the whole time. The first sign of red you sell and take your money out for a loss. Later, you realized your friends were right; you could have bought four Lambos if you had continued holding. Trading or investing with fear will hold back every trader reading this. Being attached to money can produce this emotion. Fear will hold you back in many ways including hesitation, taking profits too early, letting losers run, and unleashing other lethal emotions. There are many reasons we can be scared, but the main reason is we are probably trading with money we can't afford to lose. Therefore, it is important to correct the reason we are fearful, so it doesn't hold us back. Your goal is to eliminate all the lethal emotions listed previously so we can become robots trading the stock market. By eliminating fear, we can enter the trade without hesitation, let it play out for the good and the bad, and sleep well at night. These are all positive factors for us to succeed in the stock market. We cannot have success until we can do those exact things.

Fear in some ways prepares us for the downside. It allows us to acknowledge the downside of the trade we are in, the stock we are holding, or the money we are using. If this knowledge doesn't cripple our ability to make decisions, it is actually very healthy to have this balance while trading. In every situation, you need to know and respect the downside. This will take the power out of it when it happens, and allow you to follow the plan. I can remember the feeling before running a big race where my adrenaline and my heart rate were high. I was extremely excited and nervous for the gun to go off, excited about winning and nervous about failing. There is a balance at this moment where the fear prepares you and keeps you sharp, but if you let it go unchecked, it will ruin your performance. This overtakes your mind and leads to irrational behavior that goes against all your training. That nervous feeling also means you care, it means you are investing in the situation. Without that personal investment, you won't give it everything you got.

You won't put in the hard work and respect the plan. You are more likely to give up in life when this nervous feeling disappears. That is when you have lost the passion and drive to continue.

MONEY
MISTAKES

START SMALL

Y ou have big goals for your first year trading. They are all on paper. You have an excel sheet showing how if you make 5% a week, you can replace your salary and eventually quit that job next year. You just learned what a candlestick is, but you see guys on the internet posting profits they made in one day which equals your yearly salary. You know it is possible, so you start the process and begin the journey. You are confident in no time you will be accomplishing your big exciting goals. One major rule I learned is, any plan in the stock market never works out how we think it will. The stock market is a professional for shaking things up and punching you right in the face. You have a goal of making a million dollars, great! The stock market couldn't give two craps. It is extremely ready to take all your money instead. With this ruthless beast in front of you, ready to tear your dreams and account apart, what do you do? From what I have seen, the best way to start is small.

Like anything in life, start small and don't shoot for the moon on day one. We all hate those interns that show up on day 1 with the goal of being a project manager over the employees that have worked there for decades. Maybe your child just became an "entrepreneur" and is going to create a living for themselves making a business. They figured they could create a smart urinal that analyzes your piss and tells you your hydration levels. The market opportunity for this is in the magnitude of billions. Your child is going to be a regular Jeff Bezos any day now! Maybe your child is raising money from friends and family to start a hedge fund based on a trading strategy they came up with last weekend. The simple math says everyone is going to be a millionaire next year.

We live in one of the most prosperous times ever in history. We just printed multiple trillion-dollar stimulus packages. If you can't make money creating a business now, your business sucks. If you can't make money trading the stock market now, your trading strategy sucks. If you continually fail in this economy doing those two things, sadly, it could be the operator. But I am not one for giving up in life and ever believing that. This may be harsh, but the point is, the factors present right now makes it hard to fail as an entrepreneur or trader. With that being said, currently, in 2021, the bar for what success looks like is extremely unhealthy. One TikTok I saw today said, "If you aren't making millions doing what you love, you are making a mistake." This narrative has been around for the last 10 years, fueled by the greatest bull market in history. Social media portrays success as Jeff Bezos or nobody. One million or nothing! This leads traders to enter the stock market with the same mentality. They want to be millionaires or blow up their accounts trying. What happened to the days when just paying your bills was winning? In the great depression getting a slice of bread was the gold standard for success, and it was just so basic. If you can feed your family, you made it. It is tough for me to watch people set their bar way too high.

I saw this with so many runners in my career. They started running and thought they would be state champions their first year. They entered college and said they would have the school records in no time. The problem with aiming high is a couple of things. Number one, you look like an idiot when you fail. Nothing is worse than telling your friends and family about a big goal you are trying to accomplish, only to fall desperately far from it. Everyone asking what happened? The next problem of aiming too high is, you forget all the small steps you need to take first. You just start reaching and leaping toward the goal, thus missing it completely. Let's say you wanted to run the world record for the marathon. Instead of slowly progressing toward this world record time, you decide every marathon you run you will start at a world record pace. In the first marathon, you make 2 miles at this pace and give up; the next one, three miles and give up. Then at some point, you realize it is impossible, and just give up. You might have been able to run the second-fastest time ever if you gave yourself the chance, progressing slowly and being okay with running 30 minutes off the world record your first year; next year 20 minutes off, next year 10 minutes, next year 8 minutes, next year 3 minutes. You get the pitch. We are capable of so much more in life by starting small and then raising the bar as we go. Start out trying to be the best marathoner on your street, then your neighborhood, then state, then country, and then maybe the world! But please don't do the reverse.

Let's put this spin on trading. Starting small refers to many things. The amount of money in your account, the amount you plan to make, the amount of time you trade, the number of indicators, and more. Starting small means not shooting for the moon, but just being a student, learning everything you can before you put expectations on it. Starting small could be the goal of not losing money your first month or year. Correctly setting goals is a skill that takes time to develop. These goals need to be achievable, but far enough away you have to work for them. Once you get close, you move the bar, and you do this repeatedly, until you get that goal you wanted in the first place, the goal of making one million dollars or quitting your job to do this. That may be achievable, but it might be 10 goals away. You won't get there unless you start with the boring goal of just having 1 profitable trade a week. Then maybe next week it is two. Starting out with the right mindset is extremely important; it plants the seeds of success. Again, it all starts with realistic goals, healthy goals. Avoid being that person crunching the spreadsheet of projections on day one, that person that uses their 401k to dabble in this, that person that quits their job without any idea if this will work. The goal of trying something new in life is not only to start small but to fail small. The money you are using first will likely disappear in the next coming weeks. Trading every single day your first week can lead to burnout and poor execution. Adding too many indicators can lead to analysis paralysis. Shooting for the moon will lead to zero success. The goal for you right now on this journey is to start small and enjoy the journey of ups and downs! If you do something you love, you're already winning.

Personally, when I started trading and running, my only goal was to win. I wasn't attached to a certain amount of money to be made in the market. I didn't have a goal time to run in a race. I was a competitive SOB who just wanted to win. Having the goal of winning allows us to work backward to figure out how that is possible. For running, it was getting better at practice; only after I was able to win the workout was I able to win the race; then one day, in college, to win the region, then one day to run the fastest time in the nation (division 3 for that season). It is unhealthy to shoot for the moon, win something small at first. Get the mind and body ready to win through consistent hard effort. For trading, it meant studying for hours to find my edge: fundamental analysis, technical analysis, value investing, swing trading, momentum trading, indicator confirmation, and anything that would give the edge. Next came figuring out entry and exit, how to execute properly when you have your edge. But fixing the mind became the focus through all these steps. In order to truly win, it all starts with the mind and that is why this book is so important for you to read. You cannot win in the markets if you can't win against your mind.

ATTACHED TO RESULTS

E very single day trading, you either feel happy or sad; you're on either end of the spectrum based on the results that day. If you make money, you're a success, and you can live the rest of your day happy. If you lose money, you're a failure, and you drag that through the rest of the day, maybe till the next day. These feelings of success and emotions are extremely unhealthy. The goal of trading is to leave lethal emotions at the door and execute like a robot. But emotional swings connected to your account swings will drain you and cut down the longevity of you doing this. This is because you are attached to the results of trading. You think being a successful trader is based on profits and losses. You attach your self-worth to your account going up or going down. You attach your self-worth to being profitable. You think losing money means you're not successful. I can name hundreds of people that have failed hundreds of times before they finally succeeded and cemented themselves in history forever as an icon for us. Those who push through the garbage every single day and finally see the light at the end of the tunnel are the ones that reap the rewards in the stock market and in life. If you're going to attempt trading and give up on the first sign of money being lost, then chalk it up as something only for gamblers, you should just quit right now. You can never ever be attached to results.

I can remember as a professional runner flying out to California to run a 1500 meter race only to have the race go out too slow, the field is too crowded, having to take the lead too early, and do all the work to salvage whatever fast time we could've run. Spending hundreds of dollars to come out here and not succeed based on results was demoralizing. But I learned through running you cannot attach results to success. My definition of succeeding in that sport was totally wrong at that moment. The sad fact is you have zero control in life which means you have no control over the outcome which also means you have no control over profiting from the stock market. So if you attach this idea of success to making money you're attaching it to something you have no control over. And if you have no control over your self-worth, you're going to be a miserable trader every single day.

Here's how to frame it to be proud of yourself every single day and achieve actual growth that is something to stand behind. Instead of framing success in dollar figures, start framing success as surviving battles in the stock market. In some battles you make money and in some battles you lose money. Throughout your time in the stock market, the battles where you make money should produce larger and larger gains, and the battles where you lose money should produce smaller and smaller losses. Success in the stock market is becoming better than your former self. This means being open and honest about what is going wrong with your trading strategy. It means trying your best to fix it tomorrow. The stock market is a battle within yourself. So if you're able to slowly control emotions, build knowledge, and not repeat former mistakes, you're a success, regardless of the outcome. Being a success could simply be not losing money this month because maybe last month you lost money. Being a success could be the ability to recognize a triangle breakout play correctly. Because maybe last month you had no clue what this pattern was. So attach yourself to the progress of your trading strategy, your ability to overcome emotions, and the ability to keep learning. The results will come as long as you stop thinking about them; if you stop dwelling on them, that's when they become real.

MONEY YOU CAN'T AFFORD TO LOSE

The very first rule anyone will ever tell you about investing or trading is not to use the money you can't afford to lose. This simple disclaimer is found everywhere on the Internet and seems to be forgotten by new traders daily. It's a very important rule that gets swept under the rug with the excitement of possible profits from the stock market. If I just took out a mortgage on my house I could probably double it overnight. No doubt in my mind this could happen. This is exactly what happens in asset bubbles at the very top of the stock market, crypto market, or any asset. People are always putting on leverage at the very scariest place, where everyone can get hurt the most. This is where extreme greed enters the market, and where there is extreme greed, there's also large institutional selling. This simple rule of not investing with money you can't afford to lose will also put you in the best state of mind as a trader. A place we can operate to succeed, not being held back mentally from the importance of the money in your account and the importance of that money in your life. The reason that money is going to hold you back is that you are extremely attached to it.

Not only do you not want to see that money disappear but you can't afford to lose that money in most cases. That money might be your daughter's college fund, or could be the money you use to put actual food on the table. When you place that trade in the back of your mind, you're never gonna be able to escape that thought. It's going to be haunting you every second of the trade, whether the account goes up or down. You will not be able to act rationally when you have this type of money in your account. Being attached to money makes you more likely to make the other cardinal mistakes of the stock market that are mentioned in this book, mainly taking profits too early and doubling down on losers to avoid a loss. When being attached, it is harder for us to detach emotions because we are so invested mentally in that money in our account.

One of the greatest things I've started implementing in my trading account is paying myself when I get attached to the money. I make it a habit of only having money in my account I am not attached to in any way. If I think losing this money is going to negatively impact my life, I make sure it's out of my account. For example this year I grew my account from 40K to 200k, and I knew that I was going to have to pay a down payment for a house. I also knew I was going to have to furnish the house, pay taxes, etc. That $200,000 was money I actually needed to do this. Therefore, I couldn't operate unemotionally with this money anymore. I wasn't attached to $40,000 because it grew so fast initially. When the bills started adding up for the family, I became attached to the account much more, at $200k. I could feel the emotions inside me as the account went up $20,000 or down $20,000. The roller coaster with that was much more intense. This is why I took $100,000 profits out of the account early in 2021.

This act of paying myself is exactly why I became a trader so I don't feel bad at all for taking money out of the market. This is actually why we're doing this. Now I have my account back to $40,000, I could trade unemotionally while not being attached to this money. This simple switch allowed me to take that $40,000 to $110,000 in two weeks. This is not the sole reason for seeing almost 200% gains quickly and my results in the stock market are an anomaly. It took me a very long time to be able to do what I do now. I will say not being unattached to the money did allow me to operate robotically which did help the account grow. By being able to trade unemotionally I had my best two weeks ever in the stock market. I can tell you without a doubt I would've probably blown up that $200,000 the next week in the stock market. I've been through this game long enough. I know the feeling right before the biggest loss of your life.

When you're losing the money you can't afford to lose, you work that much harder to not lose it. The whole loss aversion psychology leads traders to act in a way that puts on more risk and loses the money much faster. This also makes you more likely to take profit earlier in a trade because you want to keep that profit. You do not want to see your profits disappear. The money in your account is so precious to you. Therefore, any profit that you see, you will guard like Frodo and the ring. The worst part I didn't even mention is the fact that because you're so attached to the money, you'll do anything to avoid a loss. There is a self-fulfilling prophecy that you're basically gonna lose all the money. You're fighting extreme psychological hard wiring in your brain to stop this from happening, the type of psychological force that is going to be impossible to control.

The very worst part I didn't even mention yet, is that when you lose this money, it affects your life negatively as a direct impact on your welfare. Whether that money was a loan, a second mortgage, your 401(k), or your life savings, losing that money can change your life for the worse. The decisions you make right could greatly alter everything. I will say this one more time. If your trading strategy is half as good as you think it is, you don't need to take out debt, or use your savings account to grow your capital. Being patient is the name of the game and you can't be successful if you are rushing the process in the stock market. That means you might have to grow $500, instead of $5000 of money you are attached to.

Personally, as a semi-professional runner, all I wanted was to run amazing times. I was so attached to running a certain qualifier, record, or just a personal best. When I toed the line, that's all I had on my mind and it's all I dreamed about on every single run and every single workout, instead of trusting the process and being smart, I let my emotions take the reins. Instead of trusting my instincts, which I spent 10,000 hours training every single day for 10 years, I said, "Screw my instincts, I'm just gonna go for it." Sacrificing many races, chasing times that were achievable in the long term, but not the short term. Sacrificing the long term for the short term, giving up a good race and chasing the great races. This is the same in the stock market; you're sacrificing mediocre gains for amazing gains, resulting in large account losses. You're putting on leverage and trading with money you're attached to instead of trading with smaller capital with smaller rewards, sacrificing the good effort for the great effort. Whenever you're reaching somewhere in life that's when you fall the hardest on your face. So stop reaching, take that baby step and be OK with being mediocre today, one bite at a time.

BREAK-EVEN

Y ou just lost five bucks in the stock market, sorry maybe $5000. Hey, I've seen some people lose $50,000. Whatever your loss may be, this is your first instant reaction from a psychological standpoint. This is something you're gonna have to fight every fiber of your being to stop, which is telling yourself you need to break even, adding on more risk and taking more chances just to give yourself a shot at not having that loss anymore. This is called loss aversion, and it's hard-wired inside your brain. Unfortunately, losing money is one of the worst feelings any person has to go through. It also creates the most intense emotion that triggers this loss aversion mindset. Loss aversion is the act of doing everything in your power to avoid the loss. For a trader, this can be done in various ways. Taking out credit card debt, calling up your local YouTube guru, joining a trading group, buying short-term options, you name it. I personally have done them all so I can tell you from first-hand experience.

Let's say I have target calls going out one month till expiration. If those calls drop 50% in value, what I could do to avoid that loss is double down here. If I double down, I can get my money back and break even much quicker, which would help me avoid the loss. I could also get out of these options and buy the weekly expirations, or the zero-day options. This would help because they have so much more leverage compared to their cost, which would also produce the same result of helping me get back to break even much quicker. In both scenarios what I'm doing is adding on the risk just because I'm losing with the idea of avoiding the loss at all costs. This is the exact definition of loss aversion, and this is what I see many traders do.

This is by far one of the biggest mistakes in the stock market for traders, not only could you break even faster, but you could also lose your money twice as fast if you double down. Let's say you quadrupled your position, if it goes against you now you're losing four times as much. I think you get the picture. Plenty of times in the stock market I've been down $1000-$10,000. I've always thought that was the worst loss of my month and it made me so angry. Obviously, no one wants to see red in their account. But the problem is, as you add on the risk, that $10,000 loss could turn into $20k, $50k, and then $100,000. Now you're looking at one of the largest losses, ever, wishing you just cut your losing trade an hour ago. Unfortunately, the act of not cutting your losses can result in a balloon effect where you end up seeing your biggest loser ever in history grow and grow. This is why I tell all my traders it could always be worse. You lost $10,000 so what. The decisions you make at this moment could put you on the path to success, and maybe get back that 10,000 or they can put you on the path to spiral out of control. In the worst-case scenario put your family in debt or blow up life savings. The decision you make when you see a loss can literally change everything in your trading career. This is one of the most delicate points in trading and you have to recognize that trying to make up any past losses is a fool's errand. That mindset will almost always lead to extra losses. The smartest thing you can do is just forget about the loss. Everybody loses money. We all pay tuition. You're not special for losing money in the stock market. Congratulations on being initiated. The goal now is to pump the brakes and drive slow homie. The goal is to wake up one day and not even think about that loss. If you keep thinking about the money you lost, you're letting the stock market win. You're letting the stock market live in your head rent-free. That's what it wants to do, to continue to take your money and put you on tilt. So you have to give the stock market the middle finger and wake up without the mindset of breaking even, with zero intention of getting that money back, because only when you operate unemotionally will you be able to execute properly and put yourself in a position to possibly make it back. So defeat that stock market demon, put your ego aside, and don't let past losses drive any decisions moving forward.

BASE HITS

You just woke up, logged onto WallStreetBets, and saw one of the users made $1 million on Tesla calls. This ignites a real fire inside you called FOMO. You wonder why anyone didn't tell you about this trade opportunity and can't believe you missed out on a $1 million trade. This FOMO leads you to try to find your own million-dollar trade, maybe 1000% winner, fueled by whatever crazy stupid trade somebody posted on the Internet risking 100% of their capital. Those trades from the degenerate gamblers have changed your mindset from trading like a robot, to going all in $1 million or bust. This is the danger of browsing social media and comparing ourselves to those on there. Overnight zero-day calls with a whole account or nothing. The popularity of the stock market has been a terrible thing for many people. Seeing others make money is not healthy for you. The feelings and emotions that are created from this are going to lead you to shoot for the moon, which leads to putting on too much risk and not playing the long game. When you start trading like this, you start forgetting the real reason you entered the stock market. It wasn't a gamble; it was to try to create a living from being patient and trading unemotionally.

I feel this all the time and I'm sure it's much stronger for beginning traders. Seeing someone else make money makes me feel like crap especially when it's an amount of money I would love to make, especially, when they made it easily overnight. I've trained my brain to subdue this lethal emotion of jealousy, FOMO, and rage. Whatever it is, and repeated this mantra every single second. It's about how much you can make in 10 years, not 10 minutes. These people making millions in a day will also lose millions in a day and you'll never hear that story or see that screenshot. If you have the ability to become an overnight millionaire you're putting on way too much risk. If this is the way you're trading your account it is most likely going to end extremely badly. It's going to come spiraling down in a matter of time, which I really hope that's not the case. This risky trading strategy a trader develops is a blessing and a curse. Well, actually it's 100% a curse. You're gonna think this is a long-term profitable trading strategy and it's gonna take you forever to find the real truth of the market. I see this all the time with new traders, they confuse luck with brilliance. They develop an ego and believe they made it, but the market in time will humble those traders very quickly. The name of the game is patience and everyone seems to forget it. Just crunch the numbers and it's incredible how much you can make from 10% a week or even $1000 a day. This greed of trying to make unlimited amounts of money is defeating the purpose of the stock market. The reason you started trading may have been in order to quit your job or pay the bills. So the simple reason you started trading should never get confused and morph into a motivation to become some ultra-billionaire with 7 yachts. Like everything in life, it's about starting small and putting in the grind daily, setting the bar low and just going through the process, not being attached to the results. Forget about the gamblers out there, showing their screenshots of making more money than Jeff Bezos. That's certainly not sustainable, and shouldn't be your goal ever in the stock market. You're welcome to have a portion of your capital reserved for ultra-risky plays. There is nothing wrong with having small capital for ultra-risky plays. From my experience in the stock market, the ultra-risky section of your portfolio tends to underperform the safer, more strategic part of your portfolio. The stock market is all about the base hits not about home runs.

The biggest mistake that led to my biggest account being blown up was trying to reach and quickly double my account. I recently turned $3,000-$45,000 and thought how cool it would be to hit six figures, $100,000 in the next 24 hours. When you feel invincible and greedy that's when you give up the largest portion of your portfolio quickly. This could be caused by seeing other people be able to do this, and now you feel like you missed out. If it's so easy you can do it too. I can assure you, starting back at zero for your portfolio sets you back greatly. Starting at zero is so much harder to get to where you were before. It could take months or years. If this happens to you don't dwell on it, accept it and move on. This is your journey and you have to own it 100% which means accepting the mistakes and having faith in the long game. Whenever I reach in the stock market instead of taking base hits, that's when I experience my biggest regrets. Again $1000 a day adds up and 10% a week has a hockey stick curve on your portfolio.

I experienced the same mistake in my running career as well. My last year running was when the coronavirus happened. All year long I had to train all by myself with no races on the schedule. Having nothing to train for was demoralizing, and many of my friends ended up quitting the sport at this time. Luckily, later in the summer, some meet directors organized a couple of races to allow some athletes to finally put their training to use. These were the only races of the year and there were about three of them. I can remember going to the first race and just being grateful to be there. I had no expectations, no motivation to hit a home run; I just wanted to use this opportunity as best as I could. I ended up feeling out of the race and running the plan perfectly. Conserving energy in the beginning, then slowly start putting the pedal on the gas each lap.

After two years of not racing, I was able to cross the line a quarter second away from my personal best. This is extremely hard to do by the way. Most runners need one whole month of racing to even have a shot of touching their personal best. I should've been proud of what happened, instead, I got greedy and I wanted more. I didn't want to run close to my best. I wanted to run faster. So I entered the very next race the following weekend driven by greed. Instead of being grateful for the opportunity, greed led me to squander it. I didn't run the game plan I couldn't have;

my mind was controlled by emotions at this point. I went for the home run, all or nothing. That mindset always leads to a dismal result, just like it does in the stock market. I walked away from that race with a result I wasn't proud of at all. Had I just used that race as a base hit I could've used this as a stepping stone to hit a homerun later. Unfortunately in life, we get tired of mediocrity. Instead of making gradual progress one step at a time, we try to grab it all at once. Giving up everything in the process and sending us backward.

TAKING OUT DEBT

S o you found the trading strategy that's gonna make you a millionaire. You turned $500 into $600. You feel invincible and you can taste the caviar in your mouth right now. You came up with the brilliant idea of taking out a loan or a balance transfer on a credit card. You don't have a lot of money, but you're pretty confident with a lot of money you can leverage this strategy to grow your account faster. So instead of $5000, you use $50,000 in your account from a small business loan. You realize your trading strategy wasn't as fine-tuned as you thought it was. So instead of realizing this with $500, maybe losing half, you're realizing this with money that's not yours. Your account is now chopped in half. You have to pay $3000-$4000 a month of this loan and you thought it was gonna be possible with this trading strategy. It's a slippery slope and keeps sliding.

Soon the whole $50,000 is gone; you owe thousands a month, which you obviously can't afford. It only gets worse from here, as the only way you can afford those monthly payments is by taking out more debt. It's one of the most brutal and worst devices ever created by humanity. This will control you for the rest of your life. This is one of the most lethal mistakes any trader can make, becoming invincible and using debt to trade an unproven strategy. No matter how good you think you got it, being patient is the name of the game. If your strategy is half as good as you think it is you'll be able to see some unreal growth in your account in the next 12 to 24 months. The simple math of compounding 10% weekly for 52 weeks with $1000 could result in $142,000 at the end of the year. So what's the rush? If your strategy works small amounts grow quickly. If your strategy is not profitable, you're going to realize it pretty soon. So you might as well realize it with a small account rather than an account with money and it's not yours.

Personally, I ended up taking out a balance transfer for a mortgage payment on a house we were going to buy. I had about two months before we were going to buy the house so I figured I would invest the money. It was around 2019 and I had this feeling that crypto had totally bottomed out in the market. I was going to buy some Ethereum at $117. I figured with this $10,000 I could double it in the next 1 to 2 months. I was correct. Ethereum went to $200 pretty quickly. But unfortunately, I don't have diamond hands to hold it. The emotions of having borrowed money I needed relatively soon at risk made it tough to trade my plan. So I ended up selling way too early and putting the cash in the bank account as a safety measure. So not only is taking out loans to trade extremely dangerous but worrying about having to pay it back or lose it, makes it hard to be unemotional about it.

As we've learned from one of the lessons in this book, being emotional or attached to the money in your account will make it very hard for you to operate successfully. You get too scared when it goes down and when it goes up. The question of what-if is in the back of your head. It is not possible to be a profitable trader during these circumstances. Just like my example of investing in Ethereum and selling way too early. Taking on debt can control your mind in the most toxic way. Not only that but if you lose all your money, that debt is going to control you for possibly the rest of your life. Once you start digging the debt hole, it has a way of trapping you down there digging further and further.

TAKING PROFIT TOO EARLY

So you spent all night charting the stock market and got your three best plays ready for the morning bell. Everything sets up perfectly, it's your entry point and you're in. Instant profits right away and you're almost surprised it was this easy. The stock is nowhere close to the profit target that you planned out last night but it ends up stalling/ trading sideways. And you start to think how bad it would be if this trade went red. You realize some profits are better than no profits. So you end up locking in your 10% gains and moving on. The next set up from your three from last night hit its entry point and you enter quickly and unemotionally. This trade ends up running in the opposite direction real quick, with 20% losses instantly. Your stop loss is 30% so you let it go all the way down there before exiting the trade. Between the two trades, your net is a 20% loss. You look back on the first trade and it actually ran to your profit target of 100% and the lethal emotions start to build inside you. You beat yourself up for not holding a trade to your plan and go looking for the next trade. This vicious cycle repeats itself over and over again as your account slowly bleeds over time. You find and enter many winning trades but you never maximize their profits. You fall into the boat of taking profit too early. You probably heard the phrase you can never go broke taking profits. Well yes, you actually can and it's a big mistake for many traders in the market. There's also a subtlety with the phrase above. You can certainly go broke taking very small profits way too quickly for your whole position size.

Personally, I've made the same mistake over and over again in my first couple of years trading, even when I scalp the market on a very quick time frame. I try to shoot for very small wins. I might do very well get four 10% winners and then later look back at the trades and realize they ran for 400%. Wondering to myself if I just held 1 contract I could've easily had a 300% winner. So the main problem with chasing small wins is when you do miss the big move it causes a severe emotional reaction, called FOMO. We all know FOMO is the number one killer for all accounts. From my experience, it is so much smarter to put yourself in the position to be in this big move if it does happen. If you take five small profits in one single day there is a very high chance anyone of those plays all run for much more, which means there's a very high chance you're going to be emotionally triggered when that happens. The swing trade or the larger time frame setup will always pay more than a quick 10% scalp. Looking at larger time frames increases the risk-reward of the play, so you can pay for many losing trades. The problem is when I used to scalp the market and take quick profits if I ever had a losing trade it would most certainly wipe out many winning trades from the past. When you're on the smaller time frame taking smaller profits, a big move in the opposite direction is hard to get out of. By the time you finally get out of it, it most certainly can wipe out many gains.

My solution to this is to have a plan for scaling out. Scaling out allows you to maximize the move and have your last position run to some extreme levels. You don't have to look back later in the day and realize you missed a 1000% winner. By scaling out you'll be able to leave some of your position on to give yourself a chance to hit that home run. Personally, I like to scale out at 30% and 50% for an option contract. I've learned to never scale out for less than that on a swing trade. That is the minimum percentage I will ever take for a profit, taking less than that, is considered taking profits too early. We all know that leads to unprofitable trading. When taking a 10% winner with a stop loss of 30%, the long-term math just doesn't make sense. I'm always going to be bleeding money in my account with that ratio no matter how good of a trader I am. So from all my years trading the stock market I've learned to be super patient and wait for that first profit target to hit, and make sure I'm not taking off too large of a position.

STRATEGY
MISTAKES

HOPE IS NOT A STRATEGY

You just bought an option expiring in three days. It's already losing money and it's down 20%. You don't really have a plan or an idea of what to do past setting the trade. So you end up staring at this trade as it loses money in front of you. You enter Market Moves' discord and type, "I really *hope* Palantir goes up." Then all of a sudden three traders type back that, "Hope is not a strategy". Anybody successful in what they do, never hope things are gonna work out. They put in the damn work every single day to give themselves the best chance to succeed. Hope is a silly replacement for putting in the actual work. Hope is buying a lottery ticket. Hope is spinning that roulette wheel. The stock market is not a roulette wheel despite everything your mother tells you. It's only a roulette wheel for those who allow it to be. We're not those people and you're not that person. You're the person who's going to replace hope with busting their butt, changing your strategy to blood, sweat, and tears.

Please recognize, if you're a beginning trader and you ever say to yourself, "I hope this works out. I hope Matt knows what he's talking about." You've already lost. Hope is in the dictionary for only those who never want to take this seriously. If you want to do this well, you have to erase that from your dictionary forever. I never entered a race hoping I would win the race. I never entered the gym hoping I could lift that weight. I never entered an interval workout hoping I can hit the prescribed time by my coach. I had pure faith in myself, during the race, in the weight room, and in my workout, that I can do what I set out to do. Faith only comes about from putting in the damn work. Faith becomes stronger from seeing results, from actually winning. But it all starts with putting in the work. You can't succeed unless you work your butt off. This means doing what it takes to be a successful trader: reading, charting, training, watching live candlesticks, reviewing past trades, understanding risk to reward, practicing entry/exit, and way-way-way more. The cycle is vicious and it's addicting and it goes a little something like this. Put in the work, see the results, and increase the faith in the process. Remove hope from the equation and from your dictionary forever.

HAVE A PLAN

I could give you a ton of examples of how not having a plan is going to blow up in your face. But I want to jump right in, and talk about what developing a plan even looks like. Anything you do in life, you have to look at the upside and downside. You have to be prepared for the worst-case scenario. You have to have an exit plan to mitigate losses. Most people trading nowadays are college kids that have Daddy's backup money if they need it. If you're reading this book, I'm assuming you have no backup plan. You are your backup plan. You cannot jump into this without a parachute; you have to come up with a plan. Your family needs to eat. You got to pay rent. You got to pay student loans. You have an actual life. You can't ruin it with the stock market. Please.

So first I'm gonna talk about the act of trading. We talked about this before in the book. Every single time you enter a trade, you have got to have an exit plan for a profit and loss. If you're unprepared, you're going to stand there like a deer in the headlights when you see a loss. If you're unprepared, you might lock in tiny profits, and over the long term, this will lead to huge account drawdowns. Having a plan of where to make a profit and where to take a loss allows you to not be surprised when the trade starts running. You'll act unemotionally and stay patient with the plan. I see this all the time, people just entering trades with no idea of what's going to happen after the fact. I see comments on videos, direct messages, and emails. "I am crying, I am down so much. The trade is down 50% Matt what do I do." The sad part is, losing money is part of the game. Losing money is your teacher and your gauge.

How else are you going to find out your strategy sucks, or realize your indicators are garbage? The only way you can ever know this stuff is by losing money. But the real sad part is. When people lose money, they see the rest of the money in their account as basically gone. They don't attempt to save money in their account because it is smaller than before; therefore, they view it as already gone. There is a weird mindset that traders think they lost everything even if they only lost half the account. This moment is extremely idiotic as they have the opportunity to take their money out of their account and save it. But when the ship starts sinking, instead of saving the people on board, they let the whole ship sink. This is why not having a stop loss or exit plan is so lethal for early traders. I hear this almost a dozen times a day. "Well I am down 80% and it's only $12, I might as well just hold it. It could always come back up." WRONG. Most options down 50% never come back to breakeven because more than 70% of options expire worthless. Listen closely here! If you made $12 in the market, I'm sure you would sell instantly. So if you could save yourself $12 from exiting a losing trade why wouldn't you. You can actually go use that money today and buy yourself something. Don't think about lost money in your account; think about the money you could save from taking a loss. Not to mention, if you finally exited that loser you now have money available to use for a trade that could possibly start making you money. The last thing traders should ever be doing is bag-holding losers. Traders should get better at bag holding winners if anything. Not the opposite.

One of the greatest tricks I learned from my running career is to spend time every single day visualizing. I carried this same habit into the stock market. Before and after I enter a trade, I will imagine every single scenario. What if the stock market tanks on Monday? Will it bounce after? Will I get stopped out? What if it runs? Will it continue? Where will I lock in profit? I used to spend months doing this for running races. I would imagine the runners around me, where I would be in the race. How I would feel, my mindset each lap. I would prepare for a fast race, slow race, bumpy race, back of the pack race, leading the race, and most of the time, winning the race. This eliminated surprises, so when the gun went off, I already ran the race dozens of times in my mind. I can remember our NCAA regional cross country meet. That year we were lucky enough to have it on our home turf, which means we were on the course every single day of training. For 3 months straight, I visualized the NCAA regional meet in every workout. More importantly, I practiced my finishing kick to win the race hundreds of times on the actual course, as well as visualized it thousands of times in my mind, finishing in 200th place the year before, dreaming of winning felt a tad unrealistic. But the power of visualization is undeniable, as I won that race EXACTLY how I practiced all those times in my workouts and my mind. I even had a tree at the spot I would take the lead and win, which was exactly what happened on the day of the race.

Seeing the power of doing this for my races, I continued doing it for my trading. I spent so much time visualizing, that I had dreams of my trade moving up or down. The crazy part is, most of my dreams correctly predict the exact movements of the stock to the precise price levels. This happens because subconsciously, it is something we obsess over. Staring at the chart for hours, visualizing future trends, our brain ends up actually knowing the most likely outcome. My best guess why this happens is because while sleeping our brains aren't distracting. We are able to think clearly and slow things down to see the truth in the stock market. Obviously, my years trading the stock market gave me this ability. But by applying the same principle of visualizations, I believe you may be able to predict stock movements in your sleep!

PAY YOURSELF

N ow I'm going to talk about trading as a full-time job. You have to have a plan for profits and losses on your overall account. You have bills you have to pay. The stock market doesn't owe you anything and you're not guaranteed a penny. So why do you quit your job and think you could make $3000 a month. What's your plan if you can't make $3000 this month? What's your plan if you blow up your whole account? That's the ugly downside. The hard questions you're gonna have to ask yourself. How can you support yourself if it doesn't go the way you think it's going to? Now let's talk about the happy upside, maybe the not-so-happy upside for some people. This is where extreme greed controls your account. You had a good month trading and doubled your account. You decide not to pay yourself. You have plenty of those student loans. You think with an account twice the size you can make twice the amount of money as before. Which means you can get to one million dollars twice as quickly. Your mind wanders, as you wonder how quickly your account can grow just from doubling it again. You start making some huge mistakes, which could be from any of the things we've mentioned in the book, and your account is down huge. All those profits you work so hard for are gone. This doesn't seem that bad. But when you're down giving up months of hard work, you don't wake up the next morning excited to trade the market. Like most of the mistakes in this book, you're put on an emotional tilt with this one as well. The result is a waterfall of more and more mistakes, all because you did not pay yourself. Paying yourself is super important in the stock market. The market wasn't designed to have imaginary numbers move every day. The only way you can make those dollars real is by putting them in your real bank account, paying off real debt, buying a real car, etc. If you need to pay for something in life, you should not let profits ride. The longer and longer you let profits ride and allow bills to add up, the higher chance you have of losing everything. Putting yourself in a very bad position where you now can't pay any bills. We always tell traders to pay themselves, and it is extremely important to do so. You quit your job to do this so what's the reasoning for not paying yourself.

Personally, I've made this mistake on my first two big account runs, as I stated previously, turning $3K into $25K. At this moment in my life, I actually would have used that money to do something. I needed a car. I needed a down payment on the house. We had student loans. But I just decided it was better to continually grow this account to the moon. I had no concept of what could happen if I didn't. Looking back I should've at least taken money out of my account and done any one of those smart things listed above. The reason being is, if you are so good at trading and your strategy is so fine-tuned, you should be able to grow that account again the same way you did it the first time. In no time you'll be back to where it was before. If you're so confident in your trading strategy it should be 100% possible. Because I didn't give myself a paycheck after these account runs I missed out on $60,000 of gains. I could have easily bought my Tesla for cash instead of taking a loan on it. But like most people in life, I got greedy and figured I'd let the account keep running.

NO STOP LOSSES

So you want to buy Tesla calls, obviously, Tesla always goes up, so there's no need to think about the downside. There's no reason you should ever see red in this trade. It should be all yachts and Lambos from here. Oh wait..what's that...down 5%. That can't be right. I'm sure it will turn around tomorrow morning. You wake up the next morning and your investment is down 70% from time decay. Well, you just made one of the biggest cardinal sins as a trader. Not planning, not having, or not even respecting your stop loss. You might be really new in the stock market and shocked at the idea of losing money. Maybe Joe from IT made $100,000 on Dogecoin. Maybe your classmate made a Facebook post about quitting their job to trade full-time. Nobody talks about the downside. Nobody talks about the major losses. It just seems that people ONLY make money in the market. That is what's portrayed all over social media, which is basically just a highlight reel of the so-called trading gurus or just normal folk buying Dogecoin. They only show the upside and how much money they made. Nobody ever shows the downside. So we never are conditioned to ever think about the downside, or have a stop loss in mind. When we lose in the market we feel like a failure. Like we can't live up to the image social media presents for the life of a trader. Not only that, but you're fighting your ego when you're losing in the stock market.

You plan for weeks, enter the trade, and when it starts going against you, your ego says there's no way you could be wrong. You put in all the work and plan out the trade. Your ego is the one thing standing in the way of you taking a loss and moving on, maybe making one of the best decisions of your week. Accepting losses is not easy; it's very psychological, it goes against the instinct of avoiding losses, which we call loss aversion and talk about in this book. The ego is one of the strongest forces traders have to deal with, it's gonna fight extremely hard to tell you you're always right, there's no way you can be wrong. The trade is going to come back around. So the ego leads you to not respect the stop loss or maybe not even plan for it. If you really put in the work there's no way it's gonna lose money. The truth is, the stock market is not rational.

Anyone can trade or move the stock against you. You have an unlimited amount of forces affecting the market daily. Things you can't even control, news coming out, interest-rate increases, or tweets from important people. With that being said, you control literally nothing, not even the outcome of a trade. You have zero clues what's going to happen once you enter it. Because you have no control the only thing you can control is your exit, which means exiting for a profit or a loss. It's so important that you plan for both. You don't want to be shell-shocked or unprepared when you're down massively. That's when your lethal emotions take over and that's when all the mistakes I'm talking about in this book come to fruition. That's when you learn everything the hard way. Getting in the habit of moving on and admitting you're wrong, is by far the best thing you can practice, even better than putting in the time charting or watching the market. Training your brain to subdue your ego and cut losers is huge for your long-term wealth.

Personally, this one thing held me back for a very long time. I would have these sporadic runs in the market, taking my account up 1000%. I'll admit that I just got lucky for a consecutive amount of trades. All it takes is one trade to go against you with no stop loss, no control, and all that hard work; all those consecutive winning trades are going to get blown away. Not having a stop loss can reverse months of progress. I can personally vouch for this fact as I have lost 2 to 3 months of gains, in just one trade. But all it takes is one big loss to say never again. Now when I'm trading, one trick I've learned to get over this hurdle of failing to take a stop loss is, have a defined max loss. For me personally, it's about $5000 to $7000 in one day or roughly 50% in one single trade. I've learned from the past if I let anything go past those levels the trade is 100% dead. So I might as well cut them at those levels and protect my capital. I've also got in the habit of not staring at losers but instead doing the work in the research to find the next setup.

One thing that has really helped my account is being able to diversify my plays and so if I have one loser and I have one killer set up I'm about to get into, I have no problem cutting a loser. This is what I call the rebound play. It's the play that helps you get over the heartbreak of the last one. The one that never called you back and decided to cancel at the last minute because they were feeling too sick. Instead of dwelling on this heartbreaking setup, it's so much better to look for the next attractive option. This allows you to unemotionally take the loss and then move on to something that has better potential. This is something I started implementing in the last year. It has allowed me to easily take stop losses faster than before. I've learned to stop staring at losers, stop doubling down. And just accept the loss and move on. This allows me to not only pay for a loser but sometimes turn a massive profit on the day for the overall account.

As a beginning trader, you just aren't gonna have the mindset to think of the downside because it's too depressing to think of losing money. But it's unavoidable and you have to be prepared for it. If you're not prepared you're gonna act like a chicken with their head cut off making every mistake known to man in the stock market. So please, please, please, understand the downside is possible and prepare yourself mentally for it. When you see your trade down by 50%, picture that right now, what does your account look like? What's your game plan? How do you feel? Get ready for that now. Don't let it be a shock in the moment; don't let the market have that power. The market is trying to manipulate your emotions to get you to sell at the bottom and buy at the top and all the dumb stuff early traders do. It's an emotional roller coaster that is very good at what he does. So take the power away from the market and put it in your hands.

AVERAGING DOWN

Your Tesla calls seem to not be going in your direction and they're consistently dropping in value every single day. You realize you have some more money in your account, and you think this is a discount, maybe a great time to buy some more Tesla calls. This is called averaging down and it is a fool's trading strategy. Buying something just because it's cheap and you're down, doesn't mean it's a good idea. You can get very lucky for a long time doing this. But all it takes is just one trade to never come back and your whole account is gone if you've averaged in everything. So it's very important to understand why this is bad and why you should avoid it. First off let's explain the two scenarios where averaging down is a good idea and where it's a bad idea. From what I've learned in the stock market there's actually a time and place to have this inside your trading strategy. But the problem is doing it at the wrong time can lead to so much money being lost.

The right time: Personally, from my trading experience, I will average down in certain scenarios and I will actually plan for this. Whenever I'm trading in the stock market, I have a defined amount of capital for a trade and there are some points in the market that are more volatile than others. These volatile times mean I can use less capital and still make the same amount of money, it also means when I do use less capital I still have a little bit of capital to use if a discount presents itself with a better entry. One example of this is trading the opening bell, the first five minutes, during this time there is extreme volatility which means nailing the best entry point is going to be next to impossible. So during the opening bell, I don't use my whole position size getting into a trade instead I use 1/2 or 1/3 of what is normal, which means if I normally trade with $3,000, I now only use $1500 or $1000. This allows me to scale into the trade with the volatility being high. With high volatility I know personally, I'm not gonna get the best entry point, but I also know I have extra cash to buy a better entry point if it presents itself. The upside of this is, if I do nail the best entry point with a small portion of my capital, I can get out for some gains very quickly.

Another advantage is if I don't nail the best entry point, I can always use my free capital to buy at a cheaper place. Now when the stock moves, I'm making twice as much because I have double the position or even triple the position. This is the ideal scenario because if I ended up buying at the very bottom, I am fully in, at the cheapest possible entry. Now it's extremely important to manage risk. This same strategy I will use to trade zero- day options. Please note, this is the riskiest time to trade options because they have no days left of expiration, which means the percent swings on them are wild, which also means the chance of you grabbing the best entry point is extremely slim. So this is another time where I will average down. The very last place I will average down is a long-term investment in my 401(k) account. In this account, I am mostly buying stocks or Leap options, so I have plenty of time to be correct and if I did the research, a dip in the stock is just a huge opportunity. With all of this being said, I am only using a portion of my capital for any single trade or any single investment. I am not averaging down with 50% of my account, 75%, or 100%.

The wrong time: As I said earlier, this is a fool's trading strategy, only if it's done in a certain way. Honestly, anything is a fool's trading strategy if it's done the wrong way. Anybody can be dumb with their money. Averaging down can be extremely risky and stupid if you have no control over the position size you're trading with. People end up losing control of their position size when they are emotional about how much money they lost. They lose control when they want to get back to break even. These lethal emotions produce actions that are detrimental to your account if the stock option never comes back. If you're using the strategy with leverage, options, or zero-day options, you can lose money extremely quickly. This is because with leverage you have a higher chance of going straight to zero. If you're averaging down with a long-term stock, the result of doing this may not be as harmful in the short and long term. Just because of how slow stocks move compared to leveraged assets, and the small chance of stocks going to zero; averaging down will likely lead to a blown-up account if the trader fails to see the actual trend or pattern developing, for example, averaging down puts on a bull trend. Maybe it's averaging down on calls on a market sell-off. Going against the market direction with this strategy is a recipe for extreme disaster for your account. Another example is buying a stock long term but you are clueless about its long-term potential, valuation, or the ability for it to be profitable. Averaging down on stocks that are hyped up, overvalued, don't give a crap about their investors, maybe stocks that never come back to where you bought them. The downside of averaging down isn't necessarily losing money, but the opportunity cost of not having your money working for you. In a long term investment account, buying a stock that is falling for months is not terrible, if the stock goes back up eventually. But imagine having your money in a stock that is going straight up for that whole time. Your portfolio obviously will be in a better place. Losing money or waiting for a stock to come back, contains a huge opportunity cost. Our motto in our trading group is to cut your losing trades, so you can put your money to work in a trade that could be winning.

The moral of the story is, the strategy works really well if you have defined parameters for it, and you use it strategically in your trading. Averaging down is extremely dangerous if you're going against the market direction, or if you keep buying a stock without truly knowing the fundamentals of the company. This can be summed up as, buying just because it's cheap, or buying just because you're losing money and angry. I could tell you a dozen stories of how I averaged down and almost blew up my account.

This is a very easy and common mistake to make, and it's an extremely slippery slope. It may not end with just your account; it could be fueled by credit card debt, loans, maybe even selling some of your personal property or cars. Averaging down can ruin your life when you incorporate money outside your account. The goal of trading is to minimize losses when things go poorly, so we have to be really careful we don't add to the losses by adding money to the account.

REVENGE TRADING

Y ou had a good last month trading and you're on an insane hot streak. You start to forget the original rules that got you here in the first place. This leads to one of the biggest losses you've ever recorded on your account. Instead of walking away and accepting the loss, you begin a slippery slope of revenge trading. When revenge trading, you continue to forget every single rule, doing things you said you never would do. You morph into a complete degenerate trading monster, with your eyes glued to candlesticks using too much position size while not paying any attention to the correct entry or exit, driven 100% by emotions and motivations to get your money back. This is very similar to loss aversion and trying to make back your loss. But one of the most common reactions to avoid a loss is revenge trading. In this book, it's very important I differentiate the two as revenge trading is a harmful beast. Which is also a natural mistake for traders, and very hard to stop when it begins. Some mistakes, no matter how much you read about them, will be impossible to avoid. There are just some lethal emotions that have a strong gravitational force and on our actions. No matter how perfect you think you are, in certain situations, you will find yourself making these big mistakes. Therefore, it is crucial you realize you are not perfect and you need to forgive yourself.

Revenge trading is a combination of many factors. Many mistakes listed in this book melted together will produce this one massive mistake. It is a combination of trying to make back your loss, not walking away, and getting emotional. This recipe is surely one for disaster. The trades you make at this moment, called revenge trades, are the ones where your money disappears the quickest from your account. While revenge trading, you tend to forget about position size and entry/exit, leading to overly large positions at the very worst places. Sometimes we're going against the trend; sometimes we are buying the chop. This is because we are driven by emotions and not being rational. A rational trader would never put on many of the trades that will be put on during this time.

Personally, I can remember this feeling and remember the exact thoughts afterward. That $3K to $45K account that I completely blew into smithereens was down 50% in one single day. Instead of doing what I should've done, which is walk away, take a week off. I spent 24 hours researching and developing an idea for a trade that I thought could win it all back, an all-or-nothing trade that would bring this account back to break even. My first couple of years wasn't perfect. I'll say it again. I did make all these mistakes and that's exactly why I am writing about them. So as I went all-in on one trade, rushing it, I did not get the best entry point. Only days later, I see that $20,000 slowly deteriorates. When you're in these moments you have to, and I'll repeat, HAVE TO, just walk away. I walk away nowadays when I have a feeling I'm gonna do something stupid. I decided it is best to take money out of the account during these times because they are usually followed up by nice account runs. So when I get this feeling I have learned to pay myself my profits. There's nothing wrong with paying myself at this point. The act of paying yourself allows you to not risk as much. You also don't feel like you have to make back any short-term losses because your account is so much smaller now. It puts you in the long game mindset where you're focused on the process again and takes the lethal emotions out of it. Just from my experience.

USE THE MOMENTUM

The morning bell opens and Apple stock takes off like a banshee, and it's up 15% in a matter of minutes. You start calculating how much money you can make if it falls back down, even half of the morning move or the whole move. Either way, your mouth is watering from the possible profits of the stock reversing. So you pile into puts like they're on discount. You buy like it's toilet paper during the coronavirus only to see the stock move another 10% higher. The stock is up 25% now and it makes zero sense to you. You keep thinking there's no way I can go higher, there's just no way. You realize the price of the puts is an even bigger discount, and the possible reversal is now 10% greater. Toilet paper 50% off during the coronavirus. You think this is the best deal that has ever hit the stock market. So you double down on your loser. Two things happen here. You either get lucky and you break even on both your positions as the stock pulls back or stock rockets higher as your account disintegrates in front of your eyes. Playing against momentum is something every single new trader does. Don't feel bad about this, it is a common instinct that we are programmed to do. There are a couple of reasons why we do it. Number one we feel FOMO so instead of buying into the trend, we try to play the reversal. Number two, when large moves happen, typically it does pull back so there is a huge opportunity in nailing this pullback. But strategically playing a pull back, by timing the top in stock, is something only master stock market traders can only come close to. It's an extremely dangerous game that has a very low win rate.

You're given a gift and if you don't use that gift, you're just asking to give your money away. The only thing we need to make money in the stock market is momentum and direction. When we finally have it, it seems all traders want to do is squander it. New traders tend to disregard it and try to do the impossible, which is trade against it. There is no quicker way to lose money than going against a trend in the market. It leads to averaging down and very quick losses. This completely changed the game for me when I was able to realize the correct mindset when it came to momentum. It's extremely simple and comes down to this, when you see something move directionally, delete the instincts inside your brain that says, let's see if we can play this for a reversal. Let's go against the trend. You need to wipe out that idea from your mind forever. You need to replace it with the thought of, how do I get into this. Where is my entry point? If it pulls back where do I enter? How much longer can we go? Go with the trend, the trend is your friend. There are many phrases talking about the trend being your source of profitability. Just because you missed the move doesn't mean there isn't more of a move left.

The very best part of a trend is it can go forever. For example, just look at the stock market for the last 300 years. There are so many idiots trying to go against the overall market trend, trying to fight an inherent bull market. Stonks always go up, right? The biggest point I didn't drive home yet is that the pullback from a trend is like picking up pennies, compared to riding a trend which is like picking up dollars. You're gonna drive yourself nuts trying to get pullbacks when they only pay, for example, 3 to 5%. But if you just road up any part of the trend you can make, for example, 10 to 30%. These are just random numbers but I hope you get the picture. It's a mind-blowing difference between potential profits. Even if you were amazing at nailing pullbacks and reversals the amount of money you can make is basically nothing compared to being in the trend. I would rather be insanely good at getting in on momentum then trying to call the top on it.

TRADING THE MIDDLE OF THE DAY

So you quit your job to trade full-time. This obviously means you're going to trade every second of the day. If you're not at your computer trading, are you really a full-time trader? So you do what you came here to do, trade the open, the middle of the day, and the end of the day. You think being a full-time trade means trading every damn second. You soon realize, after the first week, that the morning and the afternoon have the most movement, the most volume; they are some of the easiest times to make money. The money you make in the morning tends to be given away in the middle of the day. Options decay, volume dies off, and most of the running trades give back a lot of the gains during this time. So you feel like you're chasing every move in the middle of the day only to get chopped out. The downtrends are all fake-outs, uptrends reverse back as well. You're surprised at how you can't get consistent movement. You came to do this full-time, but you realize it's impossible to make money in the middle of the day. If you set your expectations properly you might be able to make it work. The reason the middle of the day is hard to make money is that the volume is so low. All you need is one news article, one Fed meeting, or one data point being released then the market will rocket in the opposite direction. Without volume, anything can happen to any single position in the middle of the day. You have very little control and very little direction during these times. But you fight on. You build your position through the middle of the day expecting the move. Then lunchtime comes in, the big boys get back from their naps. The algorithms pick up speed and the volume comes back. The index rockets higher by the second, and the volume builds into this move for the first real trend of the day. Unfortunately, you were building your position in the opposite direction. With the speed of the market moving against you, you lose massive amounts of money faster than you thought was possible.

This is a huge mistake for traders everywhere. I made the same mistake when I started trading full-time. I thought I needed to trade every single candle to be considered a full-time trader. You can make a living from the stock market without lifting a finger in many ways. You can make a full-time income with one trade a week. You can also really crush it by actively trading the market. There's an unlimited amount of ways to make money and you don't have to confine this act of being profitable to trading every second of the day. Mainly because there are four hours every single day the market literally doesn't do anything. There's nothing wrong with trading these hours. But the problem is when the big money comes in, you want to make sure you're in the right direction of it. All it takes is one big move with some big news and you could be wiped out with too much of a position. So as you know personally, I made it a rule to walk away at 8 o'clock mst, 30 minutes after the market opens. Throughout the day I may keep an eye on the market passively. So if something sets up perfectly, I would enter if it checked the boxes of having direction, volume, and a trend. But for the most part, I never touch the middle portion of the day. I've actually done a study to prove that the big trend in the market doesn't pick back up until 11 o'clock MST. I'm never gonna tell you exactly how you should structure your life as a trader. But from my experience, it's very important to avoid the chop-chop in the middle of the day.

TRADING WHILE BORED

The kids are gone, and the wife is out working today. You got the whole day to yourself, which means you can stare at the market every second of the day. You generally enjoy trading so you're pumped to have this time. With all this time, energy and focus you have a great first hour in the market. You decide to go make some coffee and relax. Triggered by any of the big lethal emotions talked about previously, you check your phone constantly. You're pretty bored with nothing to do, so naturally, you look for something that isn't there. Your boredom fuels a trade that shouldn't be made. You might get lucky on one or two, but one-day trading while bored will lead you to get crushed by the market. Trading while bored is super dangerous because it is fueled by the unhealthy lethal emotions that destroy accounts. We feel like we are going to miss a trade (FOMO), we want to double what we made in the morning (greed), or maybe we couldn't walk away long enough. Either way, if you feel as though you cannot control yourself from making a trade you need to take a step back. Put some extreme rules or systems in place so you have no choice but to sit the market out.

Personally, when I am trading, I schedule my day so there is no time for bored trading. From 8:30-11:00 AM MST, the dangerous part of the day, I have meetings, exercise, make a healthy lunch, and maybe go rock climbing. Just having something in my schedule, allows me to not over trade or trade while bored, which are basically the same. Another huge benefit of filling your schedule during certain hours is you can avoid the terrible midday chop. As we have discussed already, the middle of the day is dangerous to get sucked into anyways. So I am really benefiting my account by eliminating my time from the computer during the chop. I do run a trading group, so many traders wonder where I am or why I am not trading. But further reading this book you will better understand that controlling yourself is the name of the game. I know personally if I spend all day in my chat group, I am bound to take some stupid trades, which is probably true for anyone reading this book. We have dozens of the best traders in our group which means we get some of the best setups in the market by the minute. Which makes it incredibly hard not to trade when you see them!

The general rule is if you feel like you need to trade or you have to trade, you need a break. You might be addicted to something that is borderline gambling. The goal of trading is to have control of it. We really have no control over the trades we enter daily; therefore, it is crucial we at least control ourselves, which means our emotions, our schedule, our reactions, and more. Those are the only things holding us back from utter failure, our ability to control what we can control.

ANALYSIS PARALYSIS

Y ou went to Barnes & Noble and researched every single indicator, every single trading pattern. You understand earnings PE ratios and company valuations. You added everything to your arsenal to be able to attack the market with ease. You spent all night charting and planning for the opening bell the next morning. The plan comes together as one of your stocks enters a prime entry point. The only problem is, one of the indicators you studied is reading a sell signal the moment you're about to buy the stock. On top of that, the earnings for the stock weren't that great so the company is considered overvalued. Despite all the planning and getting your perfect entry point, you decide to not trade the stock. With the conflicting information inside your head, you never pulled the trigger. In the next 15 minutes, you realize everything worked out as you had planned, leading to missing some major profits because of analysis paralysis.

At some point on your trading journey, this will stall your execution basically to zero. You'll hesitate on every single trade, unable to pull the trigger, and the trades you do enter don't make money. Sometimes the more you know the worse off you are. This is because you become attached to the information you gained. Everything about the stock market is theoretical. Everything written may not have any value on your actual trade. As we have been saying, the market has an infinite amount of factors pulling it every single day. So a book you read written in the 1970s may be well outdated given the market conditions.

The goal of putting in the work to be great at something is to get to a point where you can instinctively act on it, without your emotions and your brain talking you out of every situation. Being able to trade off trained instincts instead of emotions is where success is really made. In the classic scenario, you already have these correct instincts but to be able to use them is the key. No matter how many books you read, sometimes the voice in the back of your head is the best guide on what you should be doing. Learning more about the stock market can actually be harmful because it can quiet these raw powerful instincts. This act alone can bring you backward on your journey. If you know anything about the relative strength index, you know it means absolutely nothing in the crypto market. Cryptocurrencies end up creating large bubbles that can stay over extended for months. If you were tied to what the indicator said, you would never be able to take advantage of a great crypto bull market. That's why it's important to constantly adjust and never be attached to the research you do. Adapt and adjust before the market humbles you.

I think this also happens to athletes frequently, which is called overthinking, getting inside your head. Sometimes the worst thing you can do is keep thinking. These instincts we are training daily in the stock market are powerful. If we keep dampening them, we are going to keep watering down the results. Some of the best races in my career were the ones where I didn't think. I did not analyze the race while it was happening. My very best races are the ones I remember floating, not a thought in my head, just feeling everything internally. At some point in the race, you feel this urge to take the lead, and instead, contemplate if it is the right time. As my coach used to say (without the swear word), "JUST F*CKING* GO." You trained yourself for months for this moment, the little voice in your head is usually right.

The biggest lesson I learned from my coaches is, whether that voice is right or wrong, trusting it is what matters. Hesitation is what kills us, pausing to take the lead in the race. That is the biggest mistake I could have made. But most of the time in those moments I just went for it. If it felt right I said F*CK IT. This same mindset is in trading. We can get in our heads way too often. Overthinking the trade before we get in, talking ourselves out of it, and hesitating to take profit. When we really just need to put in the work and listen to that voice in our head. If that voice is telling you to get in the trade, it is probably a good idea to listen to it. If it is telling you to take a profit, it is probably a good idea to listen. Most times I have gone against that voice, I have really regretted it.

RELYING ON INDICATORS

You consider yourself a collector of indicators: RSI, MACD, Bollinger Bands, and more. So you think the more educated you are, the more evidence you'll have to get in or out of the trade. You haven't really tested these indicators for the long-haul, but you believe more data is a good thing. One of your favorite plays is a MACD Cross, in this scenario, it's a bullish reading. If it was only for this data point you would hop right in the trade and go for it. This is one of your favorite readings to trade and you were given a gift of it. So you scan your other indicators, and you realize the RSI is overbought which is a bearish reading, which conflicts with your bullish reading on the MACD. On top of that, the stock just ran into a key resistance of the 200 moving average. So after scanning all your indicators your MACD reading was nullified after looking at your moving average and your RSI reading. The next couple of days tell the same story, not every indicator gives the same reading and you're never able to enter a trade. You figure it's time to add some more indicators which only adds to the confusion of this analysis paralysis.

Indicators are a blessing and curse in the stock market. In reality, relying on anything will hold you back because the market is always changing. Therefore the accuracy of the indicator you're relying on is always changing. As well as the way you look at the indicator, needs to adjust to current market conditions. The MACD may only work in a sideways market. RSI may only work in a trending market. Moving averages may only work in a choppy market. Or the worst truth that you're probably too afraid to accept is that indicators may actually do nothing. They may be completely meaningless for every single trade and set up you look at.

This is what I strongly believe, and that's why I don't use many indicators, aside from a couple of moving averages and one I've created specifically for my trading strategy. I've dropped all the famous and popular ones, like the RSI and the MACD. People might think I'm crazy, but I know some very impressive traders that have back tested every single indicator and found there's zero correlation in the readings they provide. People often think mastering indicators is the get rich quick scheme, and that this is what is going to make you successful and profitable easily. From my experience in the stock market, if anything seems like it is quick or easy money, it is the complete opposite, which means a quick way to lose money. You have to be really careful looking for shortcuts in anything in life, but more particularly the stock market, because any shortcuts taken can lead to quick losses. This also means it's going to take much longer to get back to where you were before. The setbacks in the market can really affect how quickly you can make this dream a reality, of becoming a full-time trader. You have to be careful being sold any get-rich-quick idea.

With that being said, I'm not totally against indicators. I think the best thing to do is to date them individually for a month to figure out their pitfalls and their strengths, which means not out of the gate, fully trusting the indicator. If an indicator tells you to buy, please hesitate first. There's nothing wrong with watching how something reacts to the market instead of jumping in gung ho with all your cash. Like everything in the market, it's best to be a student, and that includes studying indicators. The way you integrate them in your trading strategy might be totally different from what you read in the books, and the edge they give you might not be the same as how another trader uses that indicator.

At the end of the day, you have to honestly ask yourself, did this indicator help you make money, or did it confuse the stocks you were playing with? Did it give you conflicting evidence of what was going to happen? If it truly and honestly did not help you, you should not have it on your screen. This is what I've personally done the last couple of years trading, which is to only have one indicator at a time, and figure out if it actually made a true difference. If the indicator did not make a difference, I moved on and forgot about it forever. Trust me; everyone's going to approach you in the future with the new greatest indicator that is supposed to change the game forever. Approach this with caution, and be 100% skeptical if you're going to start using it to trade. It is best to date the indicator for a very long time before giving it your trust.

LISTENING TO THE NEWS/GURUS

Y ou turn on the latest Apple event. They're releasing the greatest product that is going to change the world forever, the Apple urinal. Your mind starts racing as you think of all the possibilities. Customize scents as you pee and built-in pee analyzer to allow you to know how hydrated you are. The Apple urinal is going to change the company and the world right now. So you jump into call options like a junkie with no plan, but you just know there is no way you could be wrong. The Apple event ends with crowds of applause and you go to check the stock which is starting to fall off a cliff. This makes no sense, why would the stock fall on amazing news. This is going to change the company, it's the Apple urinal. Because you took so much position size, your account is down massively and that's just the beginning, it's falling by the second. I can tell you tons of stories of how the news is going to give you an unhealthy bias when you're trading. It's going to sway your decision to do the exact opposite of what the market is actually doing. There's a reason for this, there's a reason why this industry is trillions of dollars. Smart money and algorithms are really good at what they do. If trading was as easy as buying calls after an Apple event and making money then everybody would be a millionaire.

There is a simple rule I realized, if your strategy seems too good to be true, then it probably is. The market will figure this strategy out and take advantage of those using it, especially if it is something anyone could figure out. But making money based on new releases obviously is not that easy and I'm sure you figured it out thus far. News has zero correlation to the stock market. If you believe that, it's a lie Wall Street sold you. They sold you this big fat lie so you could pay tuition for years and question your existence as a trader. Here's the theory, everything is already known and priced into the stock market at this very moment. Therefore, the event with Apple is already priced into the stock. So when the event is over, people take profit because historically the dumb money is going to come in after the event and buy the stock. Buying the news and selling rumors is what smart money is doing and that's the opposite of what you're doing. Unfortunately, if you're listening to Jim Cramer, you're playing good earnings on the stock, buying into bullish news, you've already lost. The whole system is 100% rigged to play your lethal emotions every moment of the market movement.

I laugh whenever someone sends me a news article on a stock. This is a market manipulator trying to give you a personal bias so you do the opposite of what smart money is doing now. For example, smart money wants you to sell Tesla shares so they release an article talking about how Tesla has major debt and will never be profitable. Once that article hits the market everyone starts selling and the big banks start buying the stock. News articles are just trying to give you a bias, to create lethal emotions and actions that benefit the big banks and smart money. Tell yourself that every time you hear the latest stock from YouTubers, social media, and CNN, they were all created to make sure you make the worst decisions in the stock market. If you come to believe this you'll probably have more success than listening to people making content just for clicks. It's all Clickbait, on every single level. It's meant to give you an emotional response to make sure you make the worst decisions in the stock market. If you come to believe that you'll probably have more success than listening to people making content just for clicks.

Getting sucked into the hype happens with everything in life. Listening to the news can also be, blindly entering trades based on YouTubers' recommendations. It could be buying stocks after hearing your friends made money from them. I am going to generalize this mistake into the category of just following blindly, trusting people, sources, and social media, just because they are currently having success. You need to be very cautious looking up to the millionaires and thinking you need to follow their path in life because it seems it is the only path to wealth. I got sucked into a multilevel meeting where the millionaire running it told everyone the stock market is rigged, people go broke all the time investing. Summed up, all I heard is, avoid the stock market, I made money selling juice that turns babies into men. If you want to be a millionaire this is your only option.

There are so many ways to become a millionaire, but that shouldn't be an end goal. It is about living comfortably, doing what aligns with your morals in life, doing something you can be great at, and doing it with balance in your life. Following and copycatting other millionaires is a waste of time, 90% of them aren't even happy. I saw this same concept throughout my running career. Let's say an athlete runs a world record and has a keto diet. Therefore you need to change your diet to keto. Let's say a coach got three people to the level you want to be at. Therefore you need to switch coaches. The lesson rings true here too, you can reach success in many different ways. Jumping to the hottest trend thinking it is going to get you there faster will only set you back. The path to success is draped in consistency so switching coaches, trading strategies, indicators, or diets will only interrupt the power of being consistent.

TOO MANY TRADES / OVERLEVERAGED DIRECTIONALLY

You feel like a kid in a candy shop, collecting the best setups in the best stocks. Your portfolio turns into a melting pot of positions. You just couldn't be more excited about all the setups you're finding in the market. So you have leap options, swing trades, day trades, and long-term investments. This is surely what it's like to be a full-time Trader. More trades equals more gains, obviously. When the morning bell hits, your eyes are like a pinball machine looking at all your positions bouncing around, positive, negative, negative, positive. You have no clue what to watch and you cannot focus on your trading plan for any one stock. So you make it easy on yourself, pick one stock, and manage that one position. As you're watching this one stock, you are also missing exits, stop losses and profit-taking opportunities on all the other positions. The real problem is the more positions you have, the quicker you figure out the flaws in your trading strategy. Taking profit too early for you winners at 20% gains, then watching the other six positions bleed into the 60% loss range. The losses are magnified as the positions in your portfolio increase. If you don't have a good trading strategy, you are going to know it quickly. More positions just mean you're not effectively managing them all. They're watering down your positive returns for the whole portfolio in the best-case scenario, or in the worst-case scenario, they're leading toward major losses in your portfolio.

The other huge mistake with accumulating a multitude of positions is being over-leveraged in one direction. You never want to put your portfolio in a position where it could lose major value overnight, and having too much position in one direction with leverage is dangerous. This could look like using margin and owning 200% of your portfolio in one stock. This could look like having 100% of your portfolio in weekly options. The more you leverage by the percent of positions that are similar directional bets, the percent of margin being used, and the percent of positions that contain short expiration options leaves your portfolio in a very dangerous place. If you could lose half or more of your capital with a stock market correction you are making this mistake of being over-leveraged directionally. These losses can occur when you make any mistake mentioned before. The only way to fix this is by having enough time on your options, diversifying holdings, knowing how to spot market tops, honoring stop losses, and having hedges that protect your portfolio. Ways to hedge could be, selling options, holding cash, buying volatility funds, put options, and more. Although stop losses could save you from having these large drawdowns, sometimes a gap in the market can blow through any stop loss you had in mind. This could happen for any single stock and at any moment (earnings, bankruptcy, or other news). This is the act of knowing the downside risk. Going through each holding and knowing the max downside. This allows you to not be shocked if it actually happens. The biggest goal of trading is to never be shocked by the outcome of a trade. Being shocked triggers other lethal emotions, which trigger cascades of mistakes. The way to avoid this harmful domino effect is to prepare for the downside mentally and effectively with the simple strategies mentioned before.

Here is another big reason why having too many positions is dangerous. Your time is extremely valuable, so you want to make sure you maximize it with the most amount of returns. All it really takes to have a good week in the market is one trade. All it really takes to have a good year in the market is one trade. Sometimes one trade, one stock, is all you need. The point is to focus on one thing at a time. This could also be biased, as I personally cannot focus when there are more than 3 major trading positions in my account. But I haven't been able to maximize gains with more than 3 major trading positions at a time. My strategy for the last couple of years has been to put all my time and effort into planning and executing one single trade. This allows me to watch it like a hawk, take profits at my planned levels, and cut losses when the max pain is hit.

I tried the strategy of 5-10 plays and unless I was using automatic profit and stop-loss orders, these plays were impossible to manage effectively. The mistakes I talked about above were the exact mistakes I made. Not only that but when students inside my trading group message me, the first thing they show me is the dozens of positions they have open. Then they asked me why they were not doing well in the stock market. One main problem is I can never comment on their portfolios as I am not a financial advisor. That is why this book is so important to me. There seems to be a high correlation between the number of positions you have, and the amount of success you have. Just looking at the raw math, if you plan one trade and it runs for 100%. Your returns are 100% on that play for the money you used. Let's say somebody in a trading group calls out another play, you chase it because you don't want to miss out. Then you take a 50% loss. Now your average return for the day drops to positive 25%. You watered down your results for no reason other than being drawn into extra trades from boredom, FOMO, greed, or jealousy. Making money is extremely tough in the stock market, but keeping money is just as challenging. Therefore, the goal is to do well with one trade at a time, as well as you possibly can, and then move on to the next; searching, looking, or trading when bored will just lead to watered-down results long-term.

PLAYING EARNINGS

You walked through Costco and there was a line out the door. People are buying pesto sauce, cliff bars, and 70-inch TV screens like it is the Armageddon. This place is churning profits by the minute from consumers being consumers. You hop on WallStreetBets and see people are making money off PTON earnings. Many bought options and the very next day they soared by 2000%, the typical overnight millionaires flooding your feed. The typical lethal emotions pump inside you as FOMO kicks in. You want money and you want it fast. You put two and two together. Costco crushing sales, which means Costco will crush earnings. Without any hesitation in your mind you buy calls on Costco before earnings, doing the math on how many millions you will make. It seems like a home run. As the market closes, you wait eagerly to see the after-hours candles for when Costco releases their earnings report. Numbers were a home run off the bat! Sales were up 10% from last year and up 5% from last quarter. Insane! You did the research, bought options, and the stock hit their numbers. Oh, if it was that easy. As you check the after-hours candles, you realize the stock is down 10%, which makes zero sense in your mind. But the cardinal rule of earnings is nothing ever makes sense, and there is zero possibility to predict the movement of earnings.

Here is why. Luckily, I have only one story of buying options before earnings and getting crushed. I say I have one story because after losing money once, I realized this was a fool's game, zero sum, long term, absolutely not a profitable trading strategy. The reasons for this are extensive but I will mention the top few. Options have a priced in the move for earnings, so you can still be correct about the earnings pop, and not make money with options. You can search these priced-in moves at www.optionslam. com. It will show you the expected move for each stock. If the stock doesn't move more than this up or down, the options won't be profitable because of IV decay. Other factors that affect the move include revenue numbers changes, gross margins changes, share offerings, dividends changes, and way more. Then, once the numbers come out and move the stock after hours, the company will hop on something called an "Earnings Call." Earnings calls have the potential to change everything for the after-hours move in the stock as the CEO will discuss their view on the company. Anything said on these earnings calls can reverse the stock after hours on a dime. The CEO resigns, future guidance is horrendous, anything. I could make a whole book on the danger of playing earnings, but I will stop it here. There are three main factors which make it impossible to guess the stock direction: the actual earnings numbers, the guidance from the earnings call, and having to beat the priced in move. I learned this mistake once in my trading career and never made it again because if I wanted to gamble I would go to Vegas.

MARKET PRICES IN
ON ITS OWN TERMS

Y ou love to find opportunities that the market hasn't figured out yet. This is called "Social Arb," and is extremely powerful if done correctly. You might have realized everyone is using this app called Snapchat. You spent some time in foreign countries last year and saw the popularity of this app everywhere. You flew back home, visited your younger cousins, and it is the same story. Snapchat addicts are everywhere in the world. This app has gone truly viral and you check the stock chart, which tells a different story. The stock is beaten down for the last 3 months as Wall Street must be failing to realize this opportunity. This is a perfect example of social arb, and this is a personal story of one opportunity I realized 3 years ago when SNAP was $13. Currently, the stock is trading at $61, which is a 400% return. Not a bad payout just from using your eyes and looking at society. The only problem was after I realized this opportunity, the stock tanked from

$13 to $5. My investment was down over 62% as I had no clue why Wallstreet couldn't see what I did while many other stocks with worse valuations and smaller market opportunities are running up 100%.

There is nothing worse than finding a great opportunity, only to have it consistently drop for months. Waiting for Wallstreet to see something you see can be very frustrating. Like Warren Buffet said, "The stock market can stay irrational for longer than you can stay liquid." This means, the stock market could go years before realizing what you see. Producing large losses on your account and if you are using any type of leverage could lead to accounts going to zero. It is extremely important to give yourself time if you see hidden consumer trends. One reason this happens is that stocks have momentum and it is very hard to change the long-term momentum of the stock. So a stock going up will take much longer to follow your bearish thesis. As well as a stock going down will take much longer to follow your bullish thesis. Algorithms follow the momentum and sometimes are oblivious to valuations and what is happening in the real world. Hedge Funds tend to follow what is hot, so they might not give any attention to the small company you found that is going to solve world hunger. Although you found an amazing reason to buy a certain stock, you cannot forget one mistake listed previously, which is not using the momentum of a stock. Just know if you are going to go against the momentum it might take a while before you make money.

The important lesson here is the stock market prices in information on its own terms. Your idea and valuation of the stock may not mean anything if the market thinks differently. When we come up with these brilliant ideas it is important to be patient and not get emotional when they don't work out instantly. If we detach ourselves from our research and being right we will be less emotional the longer it takes to happen. Like everything in trading, it is important to not attach yourself to any part of the process. This allows us to remove emotions, which leads to more rational behavior. The good news is that those who come up with their own ideas tend to be some of the wealthiest investors. Being able to be patient and see things before the market does has the potential to have huge payouts, especially when the market is irrational in the opposite direction, which could be selling the stock you love or popping the stock you want to short. This increases the amount of reward for the potential risk of the idea as well. If the research is done properly, this can be extremely profitable to traders because of these facts.

RELYING ON OTHERS

Y ou just watched some guy on YouTube make a ton of money live in front of you. You think you found the Holy Grail, as he has an alert service as well. All you have to do is sit back, wait for the text message, and rake in that sweet money. You sign up for their alert service and you realize the text messages are delayed, by the time you get them the entry points are already 10% higher. Then, when the trade is starting to make money you have no clue where to exit. The guy running the group exits slowly as it goes up, but you only bought one contract so you have no clue what to do with your profits. Some of the trades you take go straight to the negatives. In that case, you have no clue what to do either. You just saw this guy make money on YouTube so there's no way he can be wrong about his trades. You chalk this up as an anomaly, thinking that if you hold the trade, it might go back to breakeven. Maybe even a profit if you're lucky. You keep following these callouts, hoping your account is going to come back, as it slowly slips like the Titanic for the next following days.

I'm not too excited to write this chapter because I do provide a service that does this. But the lesson learned from this is extremely valuable. Every time I'm on the live stream, I make it a point to tell my traders this is not an alert service. This is not my goal when I'm running this group. I'll explain why right here. The problem with copycat traders, alert services, or CNBC hype is that you have no plan coming into that trade. You have no stop loss or profit targets in mind. When you have no plan, you have no chance to succeed, as we talked about in a prior lesson. Trust me; I've done this in the past as well. I found some people I look up to, put their tweets on alerts, and just waited for them to tell me what to look at or what to get into. I think one of the biggest problems with this is most people are not profitable traders, to begin with. These traders you idolize, the services you're subscribing to, may not have any proof of making money. I am not talking about the results from their services; I am talking about the profitability of the person running it. If that person hasn't turned a penny in the stock market, why are you idolizing them? Even for people who make a profit, they may have just gotten lucky. Real respect can be given to those who turned profits for the last 10 years. Anything less is just beginner's luck. I think a general rule is if you're going to follow someone you better be damn sure they're making money. The second important rule is, if you're gonna follow their trades and set-ups without understanding them, you're gonna fail without a doubt. You need to have your own plan and rationale for taking a trade or setup from another person.

Here is just a laundry list of reasons why you can never follow any type of service or person and expect easy money. Number one, when a person calls out a trade they don't tell you the position size. For me personally, when I'm trading in my trading group, I adjust the position size throughout the day. So if I'm trading in the morning I'm not using a lot of capital in the trade. If I'm trading in the afternoon, I might use a lot more capital in the trade. If the morning trade goes poorly and the afternoon trade goes well, my overall account could be booming. But if you did the opposite, taking a small position in the afternoon and a large position in the morning, your account could be down big. This is one of the biggest key difference-makers for traders, figuring out your position size strategy. Again this takes a lifetime to perfect and tweak. Adjusting your position size is going to have a direct impact on your P&L at the end of the day. Sometimes you might feel more or less confident in a trade, and your position size should scale with that. But that is something you can't follow in a trading group or on Twitter.

Number two, let's say I call out PTON puts in my trading group. I text out the exact option and the exact price I'm getting in. You without thinking, enter because that's why you came here. You have no mental investment in this trade; you have no idea what to do when it starts moving. If it goes up you have no clue where to take profit, and if it goes down you're just super angry you followed yet another trading guru on the Internet. Trust me; I've done this too. I wanted the easiest path to passive income. Let me tell you a secret, there is none. Passive income is a complete lie, you have to work for every dollar you get, but the amount of work you put in can greatly differ. Now, this is what happens when you do your own due diligence. That is the keyword that makes the difference between blindly following and using the information to better your trading. For those same PTON puts, instead of entering them right away, you look at your chart and realize it doesn't look too bearish. You don't see what I'm seeing. Maybe you have too many positions and you can't handle another one. Either way, you sit this one out. You watch the trade as it moves because everyone else in the trading group is hyping it up every second. You learn about that entry point, if it was good or if it was bad, and then you see it play out. What you thought was a bad setup ended up turning out to be an excellent profit for everyone in the group. Instead of getting all emotional and overwhelmed by jealousy, you should take a screenshot of that setup, put some notes on it, and put it in your arsenal for the future. So instead of following someone for a callout, you follow their mindset, and every penny you invested into that trading service builds your library of knowledge. Studying at one of the great universities we call the stock market.

Number three, somebody sends out an alert on Twitter saying they're bearish on PTON. This time they don't give the option contract they are looking at or the expiration date. They just say they are bearish. So you end up buying puts expiring that same week. You lose everything and unfollow yet another crazy trading guru. Later that month, you find them posting profit pictures of their PTON puts, as he held them for 30 straight days. 300% and they are finally cashing out. You realize you just had the wrong time frame, he didn't tell you when PTON would drop. You just assumed it was going to be instant. You figured PTON was going to drop like a rock any second now. The problem with following people online is they don't tell you the time frame that their ideas could play out. Cathy Woods from Ark Invests has a five-year time horizon. If you're buying her stocks right now, getting creamed, and decide to write off Cathy. You're making a huge mistake; everybody looks through a different lens. It's so important to figure out which lens that person is looking through so you don't make the same mistake I talked about above.

MINDSET
MISTAKES

PATIENCE PAYS

Tesla just released some bullish news and you see a tweet of someone making 10% on Tesla. FOMO, one of the big trading lethal emotions floods your system. You open up your cell phone and jump right in. Rushing the process and entering a trade without any due diligence. The trade goes up and you make 5%. You make instant profits and consider yourself a winner for the day. Only five minutes later after you exited is that trade up 150%. You repeat the process of rushing literally everything from entering to taking profits, resulting in way more losses than wins. You make $5000 your first week trading and quit your job. You want to double your account fast so you go all-in. Slowing things down will create huge opportunities for you in the stock market. It will help you avoid unnecessary losses and in time, trade much more strategically. Being patient is the trick to becoming more consistent in the stock market.

You can ask any single trader, what is the main reason for your losses, and many of them will say, rushing into a trade and rushing out of a trade. You name it. Rushing in general and not slowing things down is where all the mistakes are made. If you don't have time to even count to five before you get in a trade you're getting it at the wrong time. Personally when I'm trading the stock market if a stock not on my radar is running hot and I have to make the decision to chase or to wait. I have learned from my major losses that it's so much better just to wait. If you don't have time to plan out your entry, exit, and stop-loss with your stock and THEN wait for the perfect support resistance touch. You're rushing the trade and you're really rushing the process. The market always stair-steps with a directional run, which means a directional move is usually followed by a sideways move followed by another directional move and another sideways move, which means you're going to have a chance to enter into any single play if you hit the right consolidation. If you're not buying at a discount compared to the move or you are not buying when the move gets quiet, you're most likely going to get burned.

GOING ALL IN

So you made $5000 on Dogecoin. You passed the PDT rule with Tesla calls. Maybe GameStop brought in your salary in one single day. Whatever the catalyst is, you think you figured it out, you think you know the secrets of the stock market, you think it's all lambos and yachts from here. Then you eagerly head to your computer to type an email to your boss telling them you're quitting and hope you never see their ugly faces again. You buy some monitors, maybe the fastest PC on the market, a comfortable gaming chair, then strap in your first week as a full-time trader. All that money that came so easily just disappears out of thin air in one or two trades, as you realize you know nothing about the stock market. The market humbles you in one of the worst ways and you have no backup plan now. This is by far one of the most common mistakes I see all traders make, is thinking they are full-time material before they are. Turning your passion into a full-time gig that pays your bills and fuels your lifestyle takes a very long time. Coincidentally it also takes a very long time to develop a fine- tuned profitable trading strategy. Even when you do have that strategy and that confidence, there is a chance you could still lose it all with one moment, where you lose all control. That is why it is so important to slowly transition to becoming a full-time trader. The Barbell Investment strategy is the idea that you have a large amount of safe and comfortable stocks in your portfolio and smaller amounts of high risk/high reward stocks. In the job world, this could be seen as your safe and comfortable job taking up your whole day paired with a risky exciting nighttime side hustle that has the ability to replace your job. It is extremely important on your journey to becoming a full-time trader to keep safe stability in some percentage of your life. Mainly because it's the fuel source for trading as you find your way to profitability. You may have to fund one to five trading accounts before you find that consistency. The only way to be able to fund those accounts is, you guessed, through your stable job income. The better and better you get, the more comfortable you become in the stock market. That is when you can begin the shift of taking the weight off your safe stable job and shifting to the high reward/high-risk side hustle of trading. Just like a barbell, shifting weight should be gradual and slow, you should never put all the weight on one side of the bar. Instead, slowly shift through your journey of trading.

The reason being, if you put everything into trading and went all in, you now have the pressure of wanting to succeed and make money, which is a very dangerous pressure as a beginning trader. The more pressure and emotions you have as a trader the harder it is to execute and think rationally. Without thinking rationally, you won't be able to follow your plan, execute properly, and profit. Trading should never be something where you have to make X, Y, or Z. The goal is to have no pressure on yourself and to act like a robot. This is less possible when you don't have your stable job saving you from any mistakes you make in the stock market. I get emails all the time of people needing to do this to feed their kids or make back losses. Can you imagine a salesperson trying to sell you something out of an intense need to put food on the table? Compared to a salesperson selling something because it is their passion and they wake up every day striving to become better at sales. There is a high chance you feel the first person's energy of needing to make the sale, which turns you off from purchasing. When the second person has the energy and the mindset of wanting to make the sale, but not being attached to the outcome, there is less pressure in the situation. Just like trading.

This is the exact mistake I made in my life, but I also shifted the weight toward trading slowly and strategically. Out of college, I had two jobs that provided my income, I tutored kids one-on-one and I taught after-school classes. In the mornings I traded the stock market and trained as a professional athlete, but my first year I was not a profitable trader (obviously). In my second year of trading I was able to take $3,000-$25,000. In just two months of trading. This was definitely beginner's luck, as it was only my second year trading, and I did this rare feat in a very small amount of time. There was no consistency, and my trading strategy had major flaws. Despite all this, I typed up my resignation letter to my boss and quit my job teaching after-school classes. I was beyond excited. This job was not for me anymore. I was given a rating of the best instructor in Colorado, and I felt like I had no growth anymore. I felt as though I have mastered the aspects of this job. If you're not moving forward in your life or your job, it's time to move forward from your job. With that philosophy, I was super glad to put my time into trading.

So I ended up building out my office, double monitors, nice laptop, comfy chair, and began to make the dumbest mistakes I've made all year, but now without that nice stable income on the side. This wasn't going all-in may I add. I still had a stable income from tutoring kids weekly. I just simply shifted away from after-school tutoring, toward trading. It's important not to kill your only source of stable income while making this transition to being a full-time trader. When I ended up blowing up my account I didn't have to scramble to find another job, I just kept doing what I was doing, which was tutoring and learning the art of trading. The only downside was, I wasn't making as much now from the stable income aspect of my life. I also wasn't making anything trading in my first month as a full-time trader. This is why I decided to make a YouTube channel, just to diversify my income streams as I made that switch. Later that year ended up taking a $3,000 account to $45,000, and now my YouTube channel was starting to make some money; now starting to get a little bit more consistent and a little bit more confident in the market. I shifted the weight once more toward the high risk/high reward side of the barbell, taking the weight off of tutoring students one on one. It just didn't make sense that I would drive all over Colorado to tutor for one hour, make 50 bucks, and drive home for 30 to 60 minutes. This is also one of those tasks in life that I felt like I fully maximized and couldn't really grow any more in. I've tutored dozens of students, one-on-one and was able to successfully teach them concepts from math to science. At this point, my time was better spent on my passion and growing to become a better trader. Not only that, but when I put out a YouTube video, instead of reaching one student I'm able to reach hundreds or thousands of students. So I felt like my impact on the world was better spent making a YouTube video.

Going all-in seems to be romanticized in the society of yoloing and following your passion. In order to successfully make a living out of something you enjoy, it needs to be done extremely slowly and strategically. Again the whole goal of transitioning to doing something full-time is to never put yourself in a position to have to do this but want to do this. For example, I need to make $1000 this week. This mindset will almost always lead you to fail in the stock market and you want to be as far away from it as possible. Do you want to be at a place where you can pleasantly and surprisingly make $1000? Then one day you find yourself on autopilot bringing in four times as much as you would a normal job. When that day comes together it feels like a no-brainer to make that transition, and the best part is you don't have to do it all at once. You can go part-time at your job. You can have your wife quit her job and keep yours. There are many ways to do this, there's no right way, but there's a safer way.

LEARN ONE THING

S o you start trading penny stocks and that's your jam. You're brand new but you're getting better and better every day. You get a little greedy and you hear some people making money with options and you want in. Your consistent profits are now going to get shaken up in a whole new world of options trading. Just like penny stocks, there's a learning curve to anything, the amount of time it takes you varies based on your perseverance, your ability to learn from past mistakes, and your ability to control. That same learning curve is going to apply to options trading. So instead of doubling down on what's working and getting better at penny stocks, you lose so much money trading options. It seems like you have a good trade on a penny stock, make $100, and then switch over to options only to give it back and more. You're making the most common mistake of trying to learn multiple things at once.

This is one main mistake I made when I quit my job to trade full-time. I have the option to do this because of my success options trading. But, unfortunately, when I started actually trading full-time, I started dabbling in futures trading because they trade 24/5. Futures trading had a huge learning curve for me. Number one it was incredibly difficult to balance the fact that it trades all day long. The great thing about the stock market is, it closes on the weekends and closes at 2 o'clock MST. This gives traders some time to decompress, relax, and review the day's successes and failures. If you never get a break to sit down and reset, you're going to be running hot all the time making terrible decisions. The act of trading is extremely stressful mentally, it takes a lot of energy to stay unemotional and calm. This stress, if not balanced with downtime, creates unhealthy lethal emotions that lead to irrational trading, which leads to the inability to be patient and forcing trades.

This one concept is more than just the type of things you can trade at any moment. Learning one thing applies to everything you could do in the market: learning how to trade the open, learning how to trade sectors, learning how to trade indicators, learning how to trade candlestick patterns, etc.; the more you add, the less effective you trade and the fewer profits you will earn. The concepts you are learning, your focus, and your energy is going to get split between everything, decreasing the ability to really become great at one thing. So the best thing to do is to pick one indicator, one timeframe, one stock, one day of the week, and try to do the best you can with all of those things. Obviously, you can add more of what is listed above as you find success. I am mainly trying to drive home the idea of one. When I took my first account from $3K to 25K, I was only trading one stock on Wednesday and Thursday. I was extremely patient every single week waiting for those two days. I watched, planned, and executed 1-2 trades a week. I operated in the leanest way to take advantage of the stock market. I didn't have to watch the stocks every single day. I had slim opportunities and I made the most of them. This allowed me to make $22k in 2 months, matching my current salary that year without doing more than I needed to do. Even today, with an account much larger, I still find my best months are the ones where I focus on one stock or one strategy.

WORK IN EQUALS
RESULTS OUT

You started trading for one week and you think the sky's the limit (you may have even considered putting your two weeks' notice in at your day job!). You didn't respect this game at all. You have no clue the actual amount of work it takes to be good at this. It's like you showed up for a marathon without training 1 mile and you have the idea that you were going to finish the whole race in the first place. Later you find yourself puking and chafing only at mile number five, greatly regretting your choice to do this. Respect the market or it's gonna make you respect it. This involves studying your ass off every single day. To be great at anything in life you need to put in 10,000 hours and then some. You can't stop and get comfortable, or else the market will surely humble you.

I was lucky enough from day one to be obsessed with this. I studied my butt off every single night from the first day I found out about the stock market. Mainly because I saw the power of it instantly, seeing $50 profits into my account on the very first day without me doing anything. Just from dumb luck. During that time I was making $50 bucks an hour tutoring kids so it was mind-blowing being able to do that, making the same amount of money in my pajamas, not having to drive anywhere, and being able to be at home. Like they say, with great power comes great responsibility, so I never took the power of the stock market for granted. I knew that knowledge is power, and you had to gather as much of it as possible to really succeed. What you don't see in the stock market is what kills you: divergence, overbought, earnings reports, time decay, overtrading, emotional regulation, and so much more. These mistakes I'm listing in the book, basic patterns, technical analysis, you're oblivious to for the first year of your trading career. You're missing the very obvious and basic things that can help you succeed and the only way you're gonna figure this out is by putting in the damn work: reading books, watching videos, and watching the market as a student.

The work you put in will be reflective of the results you get out, like anything in life. So why would you ever leave your ability to succeed up to chance and by not preparing yourself for battle? This is a lifelong commitment to better yourself, and the more you know the more powerful you will be when the bell hits in the morning. From the first day I started trading, I read every book, watched every video, and watched every candlestick every single day. I still do that today, putting in the chart time hour by hour, minute by minute, and portfolio analysis daily. I realize it's so important to just keep putting in the work and even to this day I haven't stopped being obsessed with this. So don't be the company that fails to innovate and get obliviated by new technology. If you're going to be satisfied being the record player you might as well burn all your money behind your house because the only way you're going to survive in the stock market is by staying current with what is happening. You can't get complacent or the market is going to step all over you. Right now Warren Buffett is getting torn apart in this market. He has failed to adjust his trading strategy which has led him to make some massive mistakes and miss out on huge returns. What may have worked for him for the last 50 years simply is not working in this market anymore. Despite having all those years of success it doesn't make you impervious to failure. Unfortunately, he's becoming a dinosaur that is missing the bigger picture. Being one of the best examples of how, if we never change or innovate our success is going to become obsolete. I am by no means saying Warren Buffet is making a mistake, I am just talking about how in a zero interest rate environment value stocks take the back seat (nobody cares about PE ratios now), technology leads the market (which is Warrens biggest investing weakness), and when the Feds can print money all day, balance sheets don't matter. Warren's main criterion for weeding out stocks weeds out some of the best stocks of our decade because the environment has changed. The point is whether you agree or not, adjust with the environment and never think your system of trading is set.

HAVING A BIAS

You wake up in the morning, hop on Twitter, and read some more articles about the upcoming stock market crash. If you Google search those three words you'll get a new article every single day of how it's around the corner, and you have to prepare yourself now. At the time of writing this book in 2021, we've had a 12-year bull market and I have seen many people fall prey to getting sucked into these articles. This fear keeps people from taking advantage of one of the greatest opportunities in the last hundred years. This is one of the best stock markets we've ever had in history. But if you lie to yourself and let fear take over. This thought will not let you operate rationally and your account is going to be the one missing out. Having a bias that the market is going to crash or having a bias at all for that matter is greatly going to hold you back in every single trade, as well as every single investment.

It took me two years to be able to trade the market on both sides with zero bias. When I was finally able to do that the amount of losing trades got chopped down significantly. I used to fight the direction and always trade puts. Now I am able to play either direction and take advantage of the momentum. But for two years when I was trading, I never would have believed the market was going to continue higher and higher, but it always seemed to just keep trucking. Because the market was just continually bullish, I was always fighting it. This led to constant losses and small wins because I can only nail the pullbacks every so often which are far and few between. I got sucked into the same thing we all do. The stock market doom syndrome. Where you believe the stock market is going to crash any second now, and you cannot fathom any stock going up. It blows your mind when you actually see it happen and further fuels this idea of a stock market selloff around the corner.

What I do every single Tuesday and Friday with my trading group is chart the market for two straight hours. I have an idea where the stock market, in general, could go but I will take an unbiased look at every single chart to make a decision if I think it's going to go up or down. I make it a point inside my head to not let any bias come into that decision. The chart is black or white; it's either bullish or bearish. This isn't fueled by the latest news article or earnings report. The idea is to shut off your brain so you can clearly see the picture. Once you finally see the picture you can set up a trade and execute without anything holding you back. Imagine if I did this process but I have a strong bias that the market was going to rally. If this was the case I would never have found any of the bearish setups. Without being able to play both sides, greatly reduces your chances of success. Now let's say I pick one of these plays and I enter. If I had a bias still inside my head I would be second-guessing myself every second of the trade. If the stock was going up and I kept thinking about the stock market crash, I would take profits too early and get out of the play. Feeling lucky I was able to get some profits from a rally when doom was possibly around the corner. On the other hand, let's say I was playing puts, believing the stock market crash was around the corner. I would be more apt to hold those puts into major losses because of this bias. Any type of bias is going to lead to further mistakes in the market. Taking profits too early and letting losers run too long.

WALK AWAY

The opening bell rings and you make money very easily. You made your goal for the week and it's only Monday! It's time to walk away, but instead, you find yourself scanning and searching, you're still at the computer. As the day goes on you find some setups that could run for profits, but nothing is really looking great. Yet you are still here at your computer looking for the next trade. You take the next trade to only find you are completely wrong and give up all your profits from the morning. That's trading; you win some and lose some. But at the end of the day, it is all about protecting profits. So looking for trades instead of being content with your gains for the day is not the proper way to protect profits. So now you wished you walked away. Unfortunately, your goal like any trader is to make back the money you lost. This is an instant instinct that plagues what we do, created by loss aversion. So in an attempt to get that money back, you trade with way too much risk. So instead of breaking even for the day, you actually end up with the loss. This is all because you weren't content with your profits and got greedy. This greed or boredom to make more caused you to lose your gains, maybe end the day with the loss, or maybe lose everything.

Walking away is one of the best medicines for a number of trading mistakes. If you feel FOMO, walk away. If you made money, walk away. If you lose money, walk away. There's nothing wrong with monitoring the market, but there's a big difference between watching for an opportunity and actively pursuing an opportunity, searching for something that is not there; this will likely result in unnecessary losses. I've made it a habit that once 8 o'clock hits, I stop trading and monitor that last of my positions. I did not create this rule because I am a lazy trader. This is because I like my money. I like to protect my account. From my experience, if I am still trading 30 minutes after the opening bell, I am sure to lose money as my win rate decreases dramatically. I will come back later in the day to check the last two hours. Those are the only periods I actively pursue trading the market. This is about finding the right time to trade the market. This is about making a rule of how to walk away, how to pull yourself out of your emotional cave. The emotional cave that's gonna control your decisions and keep you glued to the screen looking for trades that may not be there. Think of it as an emergency release button. If you don't have one, you're going to be sucked into the market and end up making poor decisions from it: succumbing to FOMO; trying to make back losses; letting greed drive your decisions to make more money. One of my biggest pet peeves is giving up gains from the morning. I ABSOLUTELY hate losing the money I worked so hard for, losing those profits because of dumb mistakes.

I would rather have a loss in the morning and walk away and then have a gain and give it back by not walking away. Personally, it's a very strong goal of mine, that once I make money I protect that.

NOT STARTING

You spend 3 months watching the stock market, taking notes, recording Jim Cramer, and developing your fine trading strategy in your paper account. You took roughly one million to three million (paper money), and you are excited to keep tweaking the strategies. Everything serves as the green light to start with real money. You understand how the platform works; finding chart patterns, option Greeks, and your strategy makes money (theoretically)! For some reason, you don't feel ready. No matter how much extra work you put in, you still get nervous with the thought of actually putting money in your account. This is a major mistake for new beginners. The only way we learn in the stock market is not from learning from others' mistakes, not from trading paper money, but from our own money. It is calling failing forward or failing fast, and is absolutely crucial we do so. By failing in the stock market, we are able to get instant feedback on everything we do. The problem with trading paper money is that you will never feel the actual emotions and feelings of trading real money. It will just never happen. So no matter how prepared you are with your paper account, you will never succeed in trying to translate your strategies to a real account. Trading, like anything in life, is 90% mental and 10% physical. So by using a paper account to test your strategies, you are only 10% prepared for the real deal.

Let me tell you from experience, the mental game takes a lifetime to train. You never quite figure it out, and you never quite master it. So the biggest mistake you can make is not starting. Begin the journey of getting to know yourself and your lethal emotions ASAP. The longer you wait the longer you are setting yourself back. I will not sugarcoat it either. Once you start, you are going to fail over and over again. The idea is to fail as quickly as possible. Fail as many times as possible and never do it again. This will allow you to adjust, reiterate, and tweak. Then hopefully, eventually you will succeed. The reason I wrote this book is to make you aware of the mistakes that WILL be made but does not mean you will avoid these mistakes. Most people I have met in life need to make mistakes first hand or they will never learn. Unfortunately, I am sure you might be one of those people, although I hope that isn't the case.

My biggest gift in life is my ability to fail. I constantly failed in my running career, with workouts, races, and injuries. I have absolutely no fear of failing, and this really helped me accept failure with trading. If you are going to do anything impressive in life, there are going to be times you will be tested and you will fail. It is inevitable when you put yourself out there. If you wanted to play it safe, Walmart has some great benefits. It is consistent income and stable, where you don't have to worry about failing. The people who want more out of life and want to do something bigger will be subjected to the rollercoaster of highs and lows. You should welcome the highs and lows, and become more comfortable with the journey. You have to be real with yourself right now and ask yourself if you are the person made for this journey. These highs and lows can break anybody that isn't, and internally if you know you didn't sign up for this you shouldn't even start the journey. There are stable ways to take advantage of the stock market, but those come with much smaller payouts. But if you ARE ready for the journey, my best advice is to dive right in. Recognize you are strapping yourself into a roller coaster and enjoy the ride. Know it is going to be tough but knowing the end goal could be incredible.

DON'T GET COCKY

You made 100% in one single week. Everything seems easy. You got the Midas touch. Every contract you buy seems to go to the moon by some gravitational force. You start laying on more position size, instead of using 10% of your account, now you're trying 30 and 50% of your account. You figure since you're so hot you might as well use more of your portfolio. Then you have a losing trade. That must be an anomaly, you can't lose. So instead of 50% of your portfolio, you're using 75% and eventually 100%. You take a loss and move on. You've been so hot recently there's no way you could have two losing trades. Unfortunately the impossible happens and you have another losing trade, and because you have half of your portfolio in the trade your account is down 50%. You just gave up three months' worth of gains because you got cocky. Not only that but when your account is down 50% there's no way you can trade unemotionally. You're put on full tilt at this moment.

Having success is the pitfall of every single trader especially in the early months of trading. Think about it, you have no clue about anything in the stock market, and in your first week you make money. That's one of the worst things that can happen to anybody. Maybe you've been trading for one year. You have one of your best months ever. You think you figured it out. In both scenarios, you're getting cocky in a market that has a PhD in humbling cocky people. Sweeping the legs of those who have no clue what's coming. The market thrives on this.

This is exactly when I experience my biggest losses in trading as well. When I say to myself this is too easy, I figured it out. That's when the market changes everything. I think as traders we tend to forget the market is made up of an unlimited amount of forces that can move it in any single direction. Even if you have the very best setup, all it takes is one hedge fund to dump their shares and ruin your perfect bull flag. In my first couple of years of trading, whenever I took an account up 1000%, it wasn't because I was good at trading. It wasn't because my strategy was good; it was because I got lucky consistently. The type of market I was in during that time was perfect for my trading strategy. The market always adapts and adjusts to keep you on your feet. Therefore if you can't adapt or adjust, the market will sweep your account away instantly. The only way to be truly good at this is to always be on your feet and never think you figured it out. You should be always thinking about what will happen if your strategy stops working. If you got lucky for the last month you should be thinking, this is too good to be true, the market is going to humble me any second now. I remember I made this one YouTube video after taking my account from $40K to

$150,000, and I asked the market to humble me. I knew from past experience that when it seems too good to be true, the market is getting ready to teach me a lesson. When you have been doing this long enough you cannot ignore those feelings of something bad around the corner. It is actually amazing and incredible; we as traders can develop this gut feeling. It is the result of 10,000 hours. When you can be honest with yourself and know you just got lucky for too long, and that wasn't going to be the case very soon. Two days after making the video, the market humbled me. The moral of the chapter is, stay on your feet, you're never going to figure out the stock market. If you think you're going to find the trick or secret to the market, you're in for a rude awakening. Your trading strategy may have to change by the week. You may have to constantly adjust and adapt to stay alive and to reach profitability.

Developing an ego and extreme confidence can negatively affect anything you do in life. I made this mistake running numerous times. You have a good month of training and nail all your workouts. You were able to be this consistently and injury-free by getting proper sleep, nutrition, recovery, stretching, icing, lifting, and more. All the little things led to this amazing month of racing and training. Many times in college when I had these strings of training I started to think this was the norm. Getting way too confident and not respecting the process. Letting the little things slip with the thought that I could call on this superpower at any moment, and it would show up instantly, confusing luck with this superhuman feeling. Being able to will your body to do something it inherently shouldn't be able to do for great lengths of time is very much just luck. Even if you do everything properly, there are so many other factors you can't control that can interrupt these periods: the weather, sickness, life changes, and more. We do this all the time when things start going well, thinking it is the norm, forgetting the little things that got us there. Well, fast forward to a crazy St. Patrick's Day weekend, where everything crumbled in 24 hours. The day started with 4 hours of basketball, which I normally would avoid when training. The night contained too many drinks to count and a bedtime of 4 AM. The morning alarm hit at 7 AM, as many of us had signed up for the St Patrick's Day 5-mile race. Hungover, stomachs turning, we head over to the starting line, where it is 35 frigid degrees out. Feeling too awful to warm up for the race, I pop on the racing flats and head to the starting line unprepared. By some miracle, I made it through the first mile in 4:50 with the leaders and finished the race in 4th place. My prize, ironically, for being in the top 10 was a bottle of wine. Not being 21 yet, I was surprised they even handed it to me. Two days later I found myself in an MRI machine with a torn gluteus medius. Probably from basketball, drinking, no sleep, and racing without warming up. No running for 6 months, I had lost my ability to run in 24 hours of bad decisions. This is a little extreme example, but you can see how getting cocky can lead to losing everything. This happened in my running career and showed itself again in my trading career. We need to do a better job at respecting the process and not confusing luck with brilliance. The truth is we aren't half as good, or half as superhuman, as we think we are.

CONSERVE ENERGY

You start trading like you do everything in life. ALL IN! You spend every second of your day thinking about trading. You wake up before the market opens to read news articles on stocks that could move. Make your plan. The morning bell hits and you are glued to the screen for every minute the market is open. When the market closes you watch premarket levels, record trades, review the good/bad and watch CBNC or YouTube until midnight. Rinse and repeat. The process continues for your first couple of weeks of trading but your mind is growing tired. Instead of being excited when you wake up, you feel like the market is rigged. Nothing is making sense. What was new and exhilarating is starting to lose its shine. The big goals you had of quitting your job feel much further away. Easy profits become harder and harder to obtain. This is a common mistake most traders make when getting started, is burning the candle from both ends. We are not perfect and we do not have a maximum amount of energy we can expend. If we fail to realize this, we will wake up one day dreading the one thing we set out to do. We will lose the passion and the excitement, which fuel us to put in the hard work. Once all that fuel is gone, we have already lost.

Like everything in life, we need balance. For every hour we spend emptying the tank, we need to find an hour to fill the tank. I read in a book once that athletes know this fact very intimately. I personally can attest to this as well. In my running career, it was essential I found a balance. Wanting to be the best, get faster, and break records, leads runners to over-train: too much time in the weight room, too many hard workouts, or maybe too much mileage. If you never pump the breaks, your body will do it for you. Producing some of the worst injuries regular folk didn't know was possible. While running I had the option of running a workout all out, but the next workout I might drop out. I had the option of running 100 miles a week, but maybe the next month I would be on crutches. If you have too many breaks in consistency, you won't achieve your goal as quickly as you want. I had to listen to my body every single second in order to push the fine limit my body was riding daily. When I felt tired, I took a nap. When I was hungry, I ate food. Not just lettuce and peanuts, I am talking pizza and wings. When my calf hurt, I iced it and took a day off. When I ran a slow workout, I ran easy the next couple of days, Giving the body what it was craving. We all want to be great in life and achieve big things, but it is only possible with patience and consistency, these examples of running show actual feedback when your body tells you to slow down. With trading, working, or anything else, listening to our body is not as easy. You mainly don't know what to look for. That is why most runners have many injuries early because they don't know the warning signs until a couple of injuries later. It is important to listen to our bodies to ensure our longevity, pump the brakes at times, and find ways to fill the tank. Taking long extended breaks and running hot for too long makes it impossible to have a career in this, making it harder for us to reach our goals. It is crucial we find the right speed to put the gas down as well as become more familiar with ourselves in the process.

What this looks like with trading is, not giving in to your desire to think about this every second of the day. Limiting the number of days you trade, capital you trade, amount of time you watch trading YouTube videos, position size you use, and more. Trading can drain you mentally in many ways. You just need to be more aware of when it is currently doing that. The longer you go without listening to your body, the longer break you will need to take. Some ways to fill the tank of energy include exercise, eating properly, sleeping enough, meditating, and taking breaks. Just to list a few. At the end of the day, this is going to be the most personal part of trading you have to deal with. Knowing your mental limits and finding ways to respect them. What may work for some, might not work for others. Recently, I just decided to pull my profits out and take a 2-3 week break from trading. Most traders take 2-3 months. After 2-3 weeks, if I can come back excited with zero negative emotions in my head, I know the tank is full again. If those weeks pass and I am still dwelling on being greedy and making big profits, I know I need a longer break. The stock market isn't going anywhere so you shouldn't be worried if you do for a short period of time. Spend time getting intimate with yourself; knowing yourself is your goal while doing this. Any trading strategy and setup is worthless if you can't control yourself.

BULLETPROOF NEXT STEPS

OPTIONS BASIC COURSE (FREE)

Matt has spent most of his trading life mastering options. Options trading allows traders to leverage their small accounts to make some serious profit. Not only that, long-term investors use options to hedge during market uncertainty. As well as create passive income, by selling options against their positions. Those skills only come after learning the basics, and because Matt believes in the power of options so much, he decided to make this course completely free.

https://www.marketmovesmatt.com/options-basics

PREMIUM OPTION ALERTS (7 DAY FREE TRIAL)

Matt mentors and gives his best trades to hundreds of options traders every single week. His track record tops most option alert services and he strives to bring excellence to this group every second. But this group offers so much more. If you decide to take him up on the 7- day free trial, you will receive 3-5 option swing trades a week, 5-10 killer charts, text message alerts, private chat group, unlimited mentorship, 2 charting live streams, early bird discounted access to all new products, and so much more. Most traders who join never want to leave and on average stay for 4-6 months. If you want your 7 days for free click the link below.

https://www.marketmovesmatt.com/trade-alert-special

MARKET INFILTRATION COURSE

Market infiltration is an affordable starter course into trading stocks. This course takes beginning traders and brings them up to speed on what it takes to excel. Trading the stock market can be hit and miss if you don't have the right strategy, execution, and technical analysis. Luckily all those skills are inside this course below.

The sections of the course are:

- Step-By-Step Training Videos
- Secrets to Trading Like a Professional
- Trading Psychology – 5 Ways To Overcome the Mind
- How to Make Money from Technical Indicators
- BONUS #1: Value Investing Like Warren Buffet

- BONUS #2: Matt's Favorite Options Strategy

https://www.marketmovesmatt.com/
market-infiltration-training

MARKET DOMINATION COURSE

Matt constantly gets phone calls where traders ask to be mentored by him. Although he constantly teaches in his premium group, he has stopped taking one-on-one clients because of a lack of time. This is incredibly tough because Matt wants to get traders to the next level. This is where Market Domination came about; this is a 100+ video course where you can get every ounce of knowledge from Matt's mind for a fraction of the cost of mentoring sessions.

These 100+ videos take traders through:

- Indicators
- Time frames
- Moving averages
- Charting
- Candlesticks
- Options
- Entering Buy/Sell Orders
- Option spreads
- Fundamental analysis
- Technical analysis

- 10 Expert Trading Strategies
- Long Term Investing Tactics

Market domination is the most thorough trading course on the internet and the best part is, it comes with 6 months in his options trading group ($936 value for free).

https://www.marketmovesmatt.com/market-domination

DISCLAIMER

NONE OF THE MARKET MOVES LLC, ITS OWNERS (EXPRESSLY INCLUDING BUT NOT LIMITED TO OFFICERS, DIRECTORS, EMPLOYEES, SUBSIDIARIES, AFFILIATES, LICENSORS, SERVICE PROVIDERS, CONTENT PROVIDERS AND AGENTS) (ALL COLLECTIVELY HEREINAFTER REFERRED TO AS MARKET MOVES LLC) IS A FINANCIAL ADVISER AND NOTHING CONTAINED HEREIN IS INTENDED TO BE OR TO BE CONSTRUED AS FINANCIAL ADVICE. "MARKET MOVES LLC IS NOT AN INVESTMENT ADVISORY SERVICE; IT EXISTS FOR EDUCATIONAL PURPOSES ONLY, AND THE MATERIALS AND INFORMATION CONTAINED HEREIN ARE FOR GENERAL INFORMATIONAL PURPOSES ONLY. NONE OF THE INFORMATION PROVIDED ON THE WEBSITE IS INTENDED AS INVESTMENT, TAX, ACCOUNTING, OR LEGAL ADVICE, OR AS AN OFFER OR SOLICITATION OF AN OFFER TO BUY OR SELL, OR AS AN ENDORSEMENT, RECOMMENDATION, OR

SPONSORSHIP OF ANY COMPANY, PRODUCT, OR SERVICE. THE INFORMATION ON THE WEBSITE SHOULD NOT BE RELIED UPON FOR PURPOSES OF TRANSACTING, TRADING, OR INVESTING. YOU HEREBY UNDERSTAND AND AGREE THAT MARKET MOVES LLC DOES NOT OFFER OR PROVIDE TAX, LEGAL OR INVESTMENT ADVICE AND THAT YOU ARE RESPONSIBLE FOR CONSULTING TAX, LEGAL, DEALERS OR FINANCIAL PROFESSIONALS BEFORE ACTING ON ANY INFORMATION PROVIDED HEREIN."THIS REPORT IS NOT INTENDED AS A PROMOTION OF ANY PARTICULAR PRODUCTS OR INVESTMENTS AND NEITHER LT NOR ANY OF ITS OFFICERS, DIRECTORS, EMPLOYEES, OR REPRESENTATIVES, IN ANY WAY RECOMMENDS OR ENDORSES ANY COMPANY, PRODUCT, INVESTMENT, OR OPPORTUNITY WHICH MAY BE DISCUSSED HEREIN. THE EDUCATION AND INFORMATION PRESENTED HEREIN ARE INTENDED FOR A GENERAL AUDIENCE AND DO NOT PURPORT TO BE, NOR SHOULD THEY BE CONSTRUED AS SPECIFIC ADVICE TAILORED TO ANY INDIVIDUAL. YOU ARE ENCOURAGED TO DISCUSS ANY OPPORTUNITIES WITH YOUR ATTORNEY, ACCOUNTANT, FINANCIAL EXPERT, OR OTHER ADVISOR. YOUR USE OF THE INFORMATION CONTAINED HEREIN IS AT YOUR OWN RISK. THE CONTENT IS PROVIDED 'AS IS' AND WITHOUT WARRANTIES OF ANY KIND, EITHER EXPRESSED OR IMPLIED. LT DISCLAIMS ALL WARRANTIES,

INCLUDING, BUT NOT LIMITED TO, ANY IMPLIED WARRANTIES OF MERCHANTABILITY, FITNESS FOR A PARTICULAR PURPOSE, TITLE, OR NON INFRINGEMENT. LT DOES NOT PROMISE OR GUARANTEE ANY INCOME OR PARTICULAR RESULT FROM YOUR USE OF THE INFORMATION CONTAINED HEREIN. LT ASSUMES NO LIABILITY OR RESPONSIBILITY FOR ERRORS OR OMISSIONS IN THE INFORMATION CONTAINED HEREIN. LT WILL NOT BE LIABLE FOR ANY INCIDENTAL, DIRECT, INDIRECT, PUNITIVE, ACTUAL, CONSEQUENTIAL, SPECIAL, EXEMPLARY, OR OTHER DAMAGES, INCLUDING, BUT NOT LIMITED TO, LOSS OF REVENUE OR INCOME, PAIN, AND SUFFERING, EMOTIONAL DISTRESS, OR SIMILAR DAMAGES, EVEN IF LT HAS BEEN ADVISED OF THE POSSIBILITY OF SUCH DAMAGES. IN NO EVENT WILL THE COLLECTIVE LIABILITY OF THE ELEVATION GROUP TO ANY PARTY (REGARDLESS OF THE FORM OF ACTION, WHETHER IN CONTRACT, TORT, OR OTHERWISE) EXCEED THE GREATER OF $100 OR THE AMOUNT YOU HAVE PAID TO LT FOR THE INFORMATION, PRODUCT OR SERVICE OUT OF WHICH LIABILITY AROSE. UNDER NO CIRCUMSTANCES WILL LT BE LIABLE FOR ANY LOSS OR DAMAGE CAUSED BY YOUR RELIANCE ON THE INFORMATION CONTAINED HEREIN. IT IS YOUR RESPONSIBILITY TO EVALUATE THE ACCURACY, COMPLETENESS, OR USEFULNESS OF ANY INFORMATION, OPINION, ADVICE, OR

OTHER CONTENT CONTAINED HEREIN. PLEASE SEEK THE ADVICE OF PROFESSIONALS, AS APPROPRIATE, REGARDING THE EVALUATION OF ANY SPECIFIC INFORMATION, OPINION, ADVICE, OR OTHER CONTENT. LT, A SPOKESPERSON FOR LT COMMUNICATES CONTENT AND EDITORIALS ON THIS SITE. STATEMENTS REGARDING HIS, OR OTHER CONTRIBUTORS' "COMMITMENT" TO SHARE THEIR PERSONAL INVESTING STRATEGIES SHOULD NOT BE CONSTRUED OR INTERPRETED TO REQUIRE THE DISCLOSURE OF INVESTMENTS AND STRATEGIES THAT ARE PERSONAL, PART OF THEIR ESTATE OR TAX PLANNING ARE IMMATERIAL TO THE SCOPE AND NATURE OF LT'S EDUCATIONAL PHILOSOPHY. EVERY EFFORT HAS BEEN MADE TO ACCURATELY REPRESENT THIS PRODUCT AND ITS POTENTIAL. EVEN THOUGH THIS INDUSTRY IS ONE OF THE FEW WHERE ONE CAN WRITE THEIR OWN CHECK IN TERMS OF EARNINGS, THERE IS NO GUARANTEE THAT YOU WILL EARN ANY MONEY OR GUARANTEE THAT YOU WILL NOT LOSE ANY MONEY USING THE TECHNIQUES AND IDEAS IN THESE MATERIALS. EXAMPLES IN THESE MATERIALS ARE NOT TO BE INTERPRETED AS A PROMISE OR GUARANTEE OF EARNINGS. EARNING POTENTIAL IS ENTIRELY DEPENDENT ON THE PERSON USING OUR PRODUCT, IDEAS, AND TECHNIQUES. WE DO NOT PURPORT THIS AS A "GET RICH SCHEME." ANY CLAIMS MADE OF

ACTUAL EARNINGS OR EXAMPLES OF ACTUAL RESULTS CAN BE VERIFIED UPON REQUEST. YOUR LEVEL OF SUCCESS IN ATTAINING THE RESULTS CLAIMED IN OUR MATERIALS DEPENDS ON THE TIME YOU DEVOTE TO THE PROGRAM, IDEAS AND TECHNIQUES MENTIONED, FINANCES, KNOWLEDGE, AND VARIOUS SKILLS. SINCE THESE FACTORS DIFFER ACCORDING TO INDIVIDUALS, WE CANNOT GUARANTEE YOUR SUCCESS OR INCOME LEVEL. NOR ARE WE RESPONSIBLE FOR ANY OF YOUR ACTIONS. ANY OF OUR SALES MATERIALS IS INTENDED TO EXPRESS OUR OPINION OF EARNINGS POTENTIAL. MANY FACTORS WILL BE IMPORTANT IN DETERMINING YOUR ACTUAL RESULTS AND NO GUARANTEES ARE MADE THAT YOU WILL ACHIEVE RESULTS SIMILAR TO OURS OR ANYBODY ELSE'S, IN FACT, NO GUARANTEES ARE MADE THAT YOU WILL ACHIEVE ANY RESULTS FROM OUR IDEAS AND TECHNIQUES IN OUR MATERIAL.

MARKET MOVES LLC does not receive any compensation from any party in relation to any stocks or securities mentioned or traded in any of its services. All content displayed is entirely informational, and is not suggested or intended to replace skilled research, advice, or guidance from licensed investors or otherwise. All information provided is for education purposes only. MARKET MOVES LLC is not an advisory service or a registered investment broker-dealer. We may hold positions in stocks, options, and other market instruments discussed, but this in no way constitutes investment advice. All trades and positions posted and/or discussed by the chat room moderator are neither a solicitation to buy or sell a particular security or market instrument nor are they investment advice. MARKET MOVES LLC live trading room, chart examples, webinars, videos, mentoring, emails and any other content on this website is for the sole purpose of education and information, and should not be construed as investment advice. We do not provide tax or legal advice as it relates to stock trading, please refer to a qualified professional for these services. Trading the markets in any capacity involves a substantial risk of loss. This activity may not be appropriate for everyone, and you should only risk what you can afford to lose. MARKET MOVES LLC does not guarantee trading profits, nor do we guarantee freedom from risk. You must assess the risk of any trade with your broker or financial professional and then make your own independent decisions regarding any trades taken. MARKET MOVES LLC is in no way responsible or liable for any trader losses whatsoever.